Also from this author:

The Roller Coaster of My Bipolar Disorder
Autobiography

COERCION: THE ACHILLES' HEEL OF EDUCATION

SOCIOLOGICAL ESSAY

ROMÉO GAUVREAU, B.A., *Ph.D.,...in B.S.*

Order this book online at www.trafford.com
or email orders@trafford.com

Most Trafford titles are also available at major online book retailers.

Printed in the United States of America.

ISBN: 978-1-4907-4055-3 (sc)
ISBN: 978-1-4907-4057-7 (hc)
ISBN: 978-1-4907-4056-0 (e)

Library of Congress Control Number: 2014911272

Trafford rev. 06/25/2014

 www.trafford.com

North America & international
toll-free: 1 888 232 4444 (USA & Canada)
fax: 812 355 4082

*First, I dedicate this book
to my elementary school teacher, Miss Estelle Landry
who has taught me how to read and write,
to my students and to all the students
at the school of life.*

Special thanks

*To Dr Craig, Judy's son,
who has helped me with the laying out of this book,
and to my son François who has helped me
design the front cover
and has accepted the task of keeping my PC in
good running order.*

To my children,
François, Bernard and Annie,
to Judy's children, Grant and Craig,
to my granddaughter, Charlotte Nicole, and
to this woman who has witnessed my
descent in hell too many times,
and has received me with open arms
on my way back,
my wife, Judy.

Table of Contents

Preface

Like through a long pregnancy, I have been carrying this book in my heart and soul since 1968-69. In my fourth year of teaching at the Polyvalent School in Carleton, Québec, Canada, I started reflecting seriously on the nature of the school system in Canada and in Québec in particular. And naturally, the thought of writing a book on the subject came to my mind.

I am not qualified to write this book. I mean... I am not a university professor or a psychologist or a sociologist. I have been involved with the school system for close to 17 years as a student and for 6 years as a teacher. To me, it was long enough to find out that I didn't like school after grade 6 and that I loved my 6 years of teaching in spite of my dissatisfaction with the school system. Through those 6 years, I refused to do what I considered harmful to the students...and I got away with it. I quit after my sixth year in spite of a generous offer from the principal. He offered me a position as one of his assistants with double my salary. I turned him down and quit teaching altogether. I could not stand the school board's *politics*...or the coercive atmosphere of the school.

I must tell you that, for reasons I don't quite understand, I have been a non-conformist for as long as I can remember. My first non-conformist move was to abandon my courses in Pedagogy at the Montréal University in December 1960 and not completing my degree. The reason for such a *"dumb move"* was my conviction that the curriculum was not pertinent to education and was not helping the teacher in me to learn how to co-parent kids. I quit ...and never regretted it. My second really consequential non-conformist move was my *dumping* my religion in 1963. One Sunday, during mass, I was getting ready to stand up in the church and give a peace of my mind to the preacher, in the middle of his sermon. My wife, aware of my feelings at their boiling point, took my arm and said:

"I think we better go…"

And she was right. I could not continue to pretend that everything was rosy. I'm not against bordellos selling sex, but… I am adamantly against a religion forcing you to prostitute yourself and, in the process, having you *pay them …for screwing you up!*

The third time was when I started teaching and realized that the school system, far from having evolved since my school years, had become a governmental *concentration camp* of sort. The atmosphere had become more and more impersonal. Students were like numbers lost in a sea of bodies looking for their next classroom like cows looking for their stall in a barn… The higher the density of a population, the more stressing it becomes for people. When a certain space is not provided around humans, -like with any other animals- it creates a certain stress and can even arouse aggressiveness. But let us not jump ahead of ourselves…

To all of you, dear readers, who have accepted my invitation to share a few ideas and reflections through the pages that will follow, I say a heartfelt thank you. In the same manner as we're not a stand-up comedian without an audience, we're not an author without the reader. I need you to receive me; I need to confide in you and to share all these thoughts that weigh me down.

Introduction

We are witnessing the *"systemic downfall of our civilization."* And the reason why civilization is not keeping up with technology, its fast advance and its efficiency, is because of many limiting factors. Among those limiting factors, there is one in particular that has an overpowering effect on our civilization: the coercion and its corrosive effect on any socio-cultural entity.

We find coercion at every level of society. I will touch most of them briefly. It's too much to be tackled in one volume. Instead, I will be dealing with one aspect of society at length, our school system.

The whole of life is a school. We never cease to learn at the school of life, even when we're not very good at it. Life's school comes under many different entities of which the first one is the family. It's the first and the most important of all schools. Then there are kindergarten, elementary school, secondary school, high school, for most, and college and university, for some. For a majority of people, added to these, there are: the workplace, the church *and, for everybody,* the government under its multiple forms: the party in power, the avalanche of ministries and departments, the police forces, military forces down to the city mayors and councilors. Last but not least, there's the peers' school. It's not always recognized as such, but it has a strong influence on us but more so on our kids.

In the task at hand, we know the culprit, coercion, and its main source, the government and its *tentacles* everywhere in society... We know the avowed goal of the school: to educate (...*instruct*) children. We also know its *modus operandi:* having children bolted to a desk for 12 years, while trying to fill their head with information and test them on it, while forcing them into compliance.

Of all the different schools I have listed above, the kids, the family and the public school system will be the ones I will address and mostly concern myself with. If I mentioned the kids as a school, it's because each child who gets born is a model of what a genuine human being is *before coercion alienates him…* And in that way, the child is a brilliant book of anthropology!

Say brother, say sister

Will you help me
When we meet on the often dusty roads of life?
Please will you help me through the maze
That those dusty roads often form?
Through the endless paths with the ill illuminated cul-de-sacs,
Where I roam too often aimlessly,
Between those high walls offering slits of skies but no exits?
Those high walls who, too often, talk of
hopelessness, fear and despair?

Say brother, say sister

Will you help me shift my sight from those walls of resistance
Towards those slits of sky full of light and promises?
Will you show me how to decorate those walls
With arrangement of pebbles of color,
Using the mud from the path as cement to
form many flowers of many petals?

Say brother, say sister

Will you help me draw on these walls,
Straighter paths with happy destinations?
And thus help me enjoy the journey?
Remind me that happiness is not a destination,
But a way of travelling?
A journey made of moments pregnant of
anticipation and discovery?

Say brother, say sister

Will you help me shift my sight from your tired body
To those slits in your face, to the smile on your lips,
To the twinkle in your eyes?
These portals of your heart, these doors to your soul,
Inviting me to a sweet rocking?
In that refuge full of hospitality,
Help me find myself, help me find my way?
Let me see your uniqueness, your Source
energy, your divine ancestry.
Let me see the light reflecting from every
fiber of your spiritual being.
Let me reflect in these mirrors of your soul
that are your mysterious eyes.
And doing so,
Let me realize how much we're alike, in beauty,
in grandeur, in heart hospitality.

Say brother, say sister

Will you help me see all that in you, in me, in all that is?
If you do that for you, for me, for others,
You will be the best teacher, of light, of life, of
possibilities, of happiness eternal; of Love.

Say brothers, say sisters

I Love you, all of You.

Roméo Gauvreau, poem composed the morning of an event
and delivered at a poetry slam in Bali, Indonesia, May 2006

1

The journey of a title

"Each has his past shut in him like the leaves of a book known to him by his heart, and his friends can only read the title."

Virginia Woolf

This book, I'm laying down on these white pages, has spent more than forty-five years simmering on the back burner of my mind while writing itself in me. This book is disturbing, according to society which distrusts those who stray from the *"path most taken."* The first title that came to my mind in 1968 was:*"We must shut the schools down."*

From that title in 1968, it remained dormant for about 25 years. And one day, Sheila, a friend of the family, brought me a book on the American school system called:*"Dumbing us down"* by John Taylor Gatto. It had in subtitle:*"The hidden agenda of compulsory schooling."*

That author had taught for around 30 years in the state of New York. Four times during his very successful career he had received the *"Teacher of the year"* award. And very unexpectedly, he quit teaching and started touring and lecturing on what he *really* thought of the American school system. And it was not pretty. I was very excited to read his book and I was in total agreement with him. I came out of that reading more convinced than ever that I was on the right track and that I had to continue writing my book.

From the combining of his ideas and mine, the title:"*School: dumbing down our kids*" was born and remained as such until a few months ago. I started book writing in September 2010. First it was my autobiography in French which I later translated in English. I had it published by Trafford Publishing in the end of August 2013 under the title: "*The Roller Coaster of my Bipolar Disorder.*"

By the end of May 2013, I had written the skeleton (first draft) of this *present book*. It's now the end of December and I just settled for its present title:"*Coercion: the Achilles' Heel of our Education.*" After 48 years trying to figure out why we have not reached a level of civilization warranting peace among world countries and peace inside these countries, among neighbours, I feel that we have not evolved as much in our civilization as a whole as we have advanced in technology.

That *coercion would be the Achilles' heel of education* is, in brief, what I will attempt to demonstrate as clearly as possible. It's a daring and audacious assumption on my part, but one that I hold dear. And before engaging in any debate, let's get familiar with the word coercion and its different implications. As you know by now, English is my second language. It makes writing even more challenging for me... *Please* wish me good luck in this challenging endeavour and let's get down to business with the concept of coercion.

2

Coercion and the Establishment

"The principle that human nature, in its psychological aspects, is nothing more than a product of history and given social relations removes all barriers to coercion and manipulation by the powerful."

Noam Chomsky

Throughout this essay, I will often use the term establishment when talking about the governing body of a country. It's not politically correct... I know...

Most industrialized countries gauge the importance or their power by their military strike force. They flex their *nuclear muscles* in front of other countries. But let us not forget:

Coercion, not nuclear power, is the number one weapon of mass destruction in the world.

We just have to think of the USA, Russia, China, North Korea, France, Israel and even Iran -who might or might not have nuclear weapons- to understand the role of coercion in the big league of world powers. Now a country doesn't have to possess nuclear weapons *of its own* to be a formidable threat. One only has to consider the fact that China only possesses 250 nuclear bombs compared to USA and Russia owning respectively 7700 and 8500 nuclear bombs. If a country was to get condescending enough to attack Russia or the U.S.A. with nuclear weapons, it would find out fast that it was a dangerous *"faux pas!"*

If that same country decided to attack Israel instead with its 80 nuclear bombs only, they would have to deal with a possible strike of 80 nuclear bombs... plus the7500 of the USA! The same scenario arises when dealing with China. Their 250 units plus the 8500 from Russia are more than enough to annihilate their enemy ...and the rest of humanity in the process, for that matter, *themselves included!*

Let's hope it will never get to that. And coming back to our country, where does coercion start? It's more circular than linear. It looks like it starts from the government and makes its way down to the family. But let's look at it closely and see if we can find its point of origin. Most parents and teachers have themselves been indoctrinated and shaped by the prevalent culture and with the rigid perimeters of the school. Mostly everybody has adopted an attitude of conformism and subjugation. It's now part of their psychological make-up. I might sound cynical when I say these things. I seriously plan to demonstrate the veracity of these serious implications before concluding this essay.

3

Coercion and compulsory schooling

"I think schools generally do an effective and terribly damaging job of teaching children to be infantile, dependent, intellectually dishonest, passive and disrespectful to their own developmental capacities."

Seymour Papert

When we are told that our state or our province's schools compare well enough with the schools of other industrialized countries, what does that mean?

"Our School Report Cards offer detailed tables showing how well schools performed in academics over a number of years. By combining a variety of relevant objective indicators ... (we) compare the academic performance of individual schools..."

(www.fraserinstitute.org)

For me, when the only thing we can brag about, regarding our school system, is *academics,* I'm very deceived! In my scale of values, academics are far from being at the top of the list. Here's what I would like our School Report Card analysts to understand and to take into consideration:

A school system that is first in academics and second or third: in *respect of the student*, in the **quality of relation of the teacher with the student,** in its *degree of cohesion with the students,* in its *non-coercive approach with the students,*

And finally:

A school system that is first in academics and second or third in its **understanding of the all embracing vocation of co-parenting the students** *doesn't deserve the name of school.*

In the present system, we force our kids to go to school. By law, the schooling is compulsory from age 6 to age16. Most will agree that there is nothing wrong with going to school and getting an education. If the school delivers that education without abusing the kids, it seems reasonable enough to send the kids to school. My task will be to find out if the school delivers the much coveted education it promises, and, if it uses coercion in the process. And, if so, what are the psychological, social and spiritual fallouts on our kids.

Let's look at a definition of coercion:

> *"In law, coercion is codified as a duress crime. Such actions ...to force the victim to act in a way contrary to their own interests. ...The threat of further harm may lead to the cooperation or obedience of the person being coerced."*

> (Wikipedia)

This part of the definition: *"...to force the victim to act in a way contrary to their own interests"* is pivotal here to understand the ramifications of compulsory/coercive schooling. For all purposes, in our case, the victims are the students. I see them as victims by the fact that mostly, they are not there by choice. About 75-80% of them are there against their will by the force of the compulsory schooling law, and by the pressure of the parents enforcing that law and forcing them to go. This is an example of *parental coercion.* There are many others as we will see. How could it be contrary to their own interests?

The answer to that short but extremely volatile question is-I maintain- contained in the book you are holding in your hands.

> *"Do not train a child to learn by force or harshness; but direct them to it by what amuses their minds, so that you may be better able to discover with accuracy the peculiar bent of the genius of each."*

> Plato (348-428 BC...)

Basically everybody knows of Plato and how wise a philosopher he was. He lived over 2400 years ago and his philosophy still makes more sense than the one of most of today's philosophers. He left us with a lot of wisdom. We use some of it in our every day conversations. These pearls are an example of it:

"Necessity is the mother of invention." And: *"Beauty lies in the eyes of the beholder",* and many more.

He clearly means that we can't transmit knowledge to people using coercion. We can force them to sit quiet and pretend to listen; but that's all.

In my attempt to demonstrate that school uses coercion as a way of controlling the students and forcing them into obedience, which is a form of subjugation, -short of saying a form of bullying-, I will try to be fair to teachers and school principals. I will try to underline the fact that the principals and the teachers get caught in the iron grips of a system designed over 150 years ago by a government that had *training* in mind; *not education.* That was the legalization of compulsory schooling by the American government, which was adopted by Canada not long after.

We must remember that teaching is a government job and that the school system is a government department and that the school boards are satellite governments, each administering the schools of their territory. By reading the next quote, you'll find out what I *really* think of the school boards…

"In the first place God made idiots. That was for practice. Then he made school boards."

Mark Twain

Because of the nature of compulsory schooling, we can observe …"*the act of coercing, use of force or intimidation to obtain compliance…*" The use of force is less and less frequent than it was in my time, but it still exists in lots of countries *"The use of intimidation to obtain compliance"* on the other hand is the backbone of our school system, (of *some of our churches,*) and of *all governments, military and policing forces in the world.* And one cannot talk about coercion without talking about power, from the prime minister down to the single parent.

"Power may comprise anything that establishes and maintains the control of man over man. Thus power covers all social relationships, which serve that end, from physical violence to the most subtle psychological ties by which one mind controls another."

Hans Morgenthau

What can we do about coercion in our society?

I'm not sure that realistically we can force the establishment to change the rules of their game. For one, to force them would require coercion which we're trying to convince them to abstain from… It is self-defeating and illogical. I would rather try, by education, to de-program people at the bottom of the chain of command,-you and me,-from the indoctrination we have been subjected to throughout our whole life.

And one of the ways to realize that goal is to help people realize that we have **all** been indoctrinated and coerced from a very young age by all our sacred institutions, family included, in most cases. And we do that by refusing to be the recipient of any more indoctrination, would it be from the Queen, our prime minister *or the Pope!* Eventually, it would bring about a great societal renewal of these institutions, of our role in society and in the level of respect of self and of others we would reach

Writing books on the subject, writing blogs and posts on the internet would, at some degree, help us educate and inform ourselves and others on the issue of coercion and its capital role *in the derailing of human affairs on the path of re-civilization.* It took the school, the church and the government over 150 years to subjugate people to this extreme. Reversing the steam will not happen overnight! But if we don't try, millions of our kids will continue to be victims of coercive indoctrination via educational mumbo jumbo. *So, for me, the school is the first place where to start, with the collaboration of the parents.*

It will be an uphill battle against the culture but I don't know of any other way or any other place where to start than in the school. One day, around 1880, while Edison was trying to find a better filament for his incandescent light bulb, one of his helpers told him:

-"Mr. Edison, you have tried over a 1000 times to find a proper filament and failed. Don't you think you should give up?"

Mr. Edison replied:

-"I now know a 1000 ways that don't work. I should find the right way very soon."

And as the story goes, the next trial was successful. So we have to keep trying because it's as worthy a cause as we can possibly tackle and also because helping our fellow man is helping us both to self-actualize in the great school of life where the soul's journey is more important than money, power and mundane success combined!

> *"A child whose life is full of the threat and fear of punishment is locked into babyhood. There is no way for him to grow up, to learn to take responsibility for his life and acts."*
>
> John Holt

4

School: What is it?

"No one believes anymore that scientists are trained in science classes or politicians in civics classes or poets in English classes. The truth is that schools don't really teach anything except how to obey orders." (Author's emphasis)

John Taylor Gatto

When we hear the word school, the picture of a building appears on the desktop of our mind. That's where we keep all the pictures forming our *"picture album"* which Dr Glasser talks about in *Control Theory*. We remember going to school as going to a place where we were forced to sit straight and quiet and, for most of us, to listen to a litany of boring subjects for *an eternity* each day.

And, in that building, we were addressed not as people or kids or friends but as:

-*"Class! Class Do this. Or, Class! Do that!" Or more often:*
-*"You! Turn around! Sit straight and shut up!!!"*

For most people from the industrial world, that picture of a building evokes a kind of jail where you had to spend 10 or 12 years of your childhood because you were sent there. You were too young to choose it when you started and... it was too late to stop when you found out what it was like and that you hated it.

In lots of ways, it was a half-disguised concentration camp. You were grouped artificially by age and often by sex in sub-schools called: classes.

To some people it does not seem to matter that we do that to their kids. To others, it does matter, but they don't know what they could do about it. I admit it's not easy to fight the establishment. Bigger a mountain to conquer than the establishment is the *milieu* or the social indoctrination level setting the tone for society's conduct. And looking up the etymology of the word school, I found out that: *"...it is derived from the ancient Greek word, Skhole, which meant either leisure, or the things done in one's leisure time, or the place where one spent one's leisure time"* (Answers, website.)

And to further clarify the etymology of the word "school":

> "...**in the most ancient Greek (it) was "time held for yourself," that is, leisure time to use for learning important life insights, not job skills, but learning you chose to help you understand who you were and who you might become in an examined life."**
>
> Bill Casselman, *On Twitter*

In other words, to get to know yourself and to reach self-actualization!

In our coercive way of dealing with our kids, a majority of us use corporal punishment. Some use weapons to discipline their kids like lots of humans do across the world with whips, belts, bamboo sticks and a whole arsenal of weapons. As a rule, we don't like the use of the word *weapon* to describe the extension of our hand for what we call corporal punishment. But let us not be afraid of words.

Not wanting to risk talking through my hat, I checked the web to see what the situation is in the world concerning corporal punishment. Here's an excerpt of it if you want to know more.

CHAPEL HILL, NC — Spanking has declined in the U.S. since 1975 but *"nearly 80 percent of preschool children are still disciplined in this fashion. ...it remains common worldwide, despite bans on corporal punishment that have been adopted in 24 countries since 1979."*

It is hard to believe that the use of corporal punishment is still that prevalent. And Dr. Desmond Runyan, MD, DrPH, professor of social medicine at UNC and lead author of a study that conducted surveys in Egypt, India, Chile, the Philippines, Brazil and the U.S. to track international variations in corporal punishment adds:

> *"...The findings are stark. Harsh treatment of children was epidemic in all communities. Our data support the conclusions that maltreatment occurs in all nations."*

Dr. Desmond Runyan,

5

Education, what is it?

"If we had in this room a hundred teachers, good teachers from good schools, and asked them to define the word education, there would be very little general agreement."

William Glasser

If we refer to the etymology of the word education, we find that "it comes from the latin *educare*"bring up, rear, educate," which is related to *educere* "bring out," from *ex-* "out" + *ducere* "to lead"

This could either be interpreted as "*to lead a person out of ignorance*" or "*to bring out a person's **innate intelligence**." (answers.yahoo.com)*

Without hesitation, I would opt for the second interpretation: "*to bring out a person's innate intelligence*". And the reason for that choice is that I don't believe we can lead our kids out of ignorance. First our kids are not ignorant. Our education system *makes them ignorant.*

To find new diamonds, one has to dig in the ground and harvest a certain kind of mineral called gangue. In that gangue or attached to it, one sometimes finds a diamond. In order to see its type and size, one must separate the rough diamond from the gangue. Then it's the turn of an expert diamond cutter to take out of that diamond in the rough the best possible

13

shape and brilliance. Like the sculpture of a beautiful woman is already in the stone, the shape and the brilliance of your diamond is already in the gangue.

In the same way, the brilliance and the humanity are already in the child at birth. They need to be led out by exposing the child to an environment propitious to his discovery of self, of the creation and of their inter-connection. To educate our children, the teacher has to bring to the table a good dose of integrity, curiosity, enthusiasm, an attitude of cooperation and openness, a capacity for marveling and a ton of unconditional love of the kids; this presupposes his love of self.

We have been duped by our teachers, by the media, by our governments, by our peers into believing that our school system was a condition *"sine qua non"* to our succeeding in life. We have been brainwashed into believing that without a grade 12 diploma, we would amount to nothing and we would never be happy! But all that false indoctrination was *delivered to us with an overdose of the most potent poison on earth:* **coercion!**

> *"Every single major push in education has made it worse and right now it's really bad because everything we've done is de-humanizing education. It's destroying the possibility of the teacher and the student having a warm, friendly, intellectual relationship."*
>
> William Glasser

Compulsory schooling started around 1855. Is it to say that the people having lived before that were uneducated? Has the last century produced any philosopher equal or better than Plato? Any musician prodigy better than Mozart? Any painter or scientist equal or better than Leonardo Da Vinci? What about Archimedes, Aristotle, Euclid, Sir Isaac Newton, Renée Descartes, Marie Curie, Pythagoras, Sophie Germain and Blaise Pascal?

Today's advanced technology has only been made possible for the twentieth century engineers, architects and inventors because of what had been realized by the people who came before us and before compulsory schooling... And the incredible advancement in cybernetics of the last 50 years pale in comparison with the advancement of the coming 10 years! Seems impossible? The more you advance in technology and gadgets, the more you have experience and knowledge and refined tools to make bigger strides in connecting with the laws of eternal creation.

I believe that it is likely that, along the ages, we might have been helped by aliens and paranormal interactions. The best example of that is the Edgar Cayce material which reveals how the pyramids of Egypt were built and the thousands of hours of information concerning Atlantis, the lost continent. Added to that, we can read material about food, medicine and a multitude of interesting subjects, for those who believe that there's a lot more to the past that *what we have been coaxed* into believing.

The question remains: do our children receive an education from our actual school system? The general consensus is: a certain amount of education. I will try to share as clearly as I can my thoughts on the contentious subject.

> *"Education is not the piling on of learning, information, data, facts, skills, or abilities -that's training or instruction- but is rather making visible what is hidden as a seed."*
>
> Thomas Moore

Through P.E. and through extracurricular activities, depending on the attitude of the teacher, there could be some education, some time. As for instruction, after the study of the three "Rs", the amount of usable information is very debatable. And we have to put that in the balance with the extremely detrimental repercussions of the coercive school atmosphere. I definitively give a thumb down to our education system. If I had school age kids, I would do everything in my power not to submit them to that corrosive influence.

6

Introduction to school

"What you leave behind is not what is engraved in stone monuments, but what is woven into the lives of others.

Pericles

Nowadays, more and more kids start their school experience by going to kindergarten. How much it helps them depends on how much we have helped our kid grow normally and develop his socialization and autonomy. And on the other hand, it depends on the maternal instinct of the kindergarten staff and the policies of the establishment. The kids usually enter that first school between the ages of 3 and 5. In this way, the transition from the family life to the school life is smoother than in my time. The sociological and psychological shock of this very important event in the life of our kids is a lot less traumatic than starting in grade one in a big alienating and impersonal school with a work program and strict rules.

Taken away from the psychological and social cocoon that family represents, the child finds himself in an expanded social surrounding in which he has to be introduced very carefully and slowly if we don't want to overwhelm him. Until then, every new situation he has encountered was in the presence of and with the safety net provided by his mother or his father or both. This time, the rules of the game have been changed.

For the first time in his life, he cannot run to his parents for comfort. If the relationship between him and the kindergarten babysitter/teacher has not been established and developed, we have a potentially destructive -even explosive- situation. It's his first experience at flying solo in society, and if he doesn't have a motherly flying instructor, he risks crashing emotionally.

In ideal conditions, if the socialization of the child is normal for his age, and he is ready for that social tsunami, he should transition well enough to prosper face to this monumental change in his life. It *might* help him acquire a greater autonomy and independence necessary for his normal personal and social growth.

We should never forget that even if the introduction to the kindergarten seems only natural to us, for our kid, it's a very important step. He might be looking forward to it if you have helped him properly in honing his social skills since the age of two or earlier. If not, it might seem terrifying in his mind. We must therefore introduce our kid to it gradually. We must never dump him there and leave under the pretense that he'll be ok and that the staff knows what they're doing, and that he is not worse than the others, and blah, blah, blah. That, for me, is child abandonment and should be avoided at all cost.

If our child doesn't feel secure at his first visit, it is highly recommended that we stay with him long enough for him to connect with that new place and with some other kid or kids and for us to know that he feels secure. Otherwise we should take him back home and try again another day until he adapts to that new family, that new world, and enjoys it. The child doesn't have to satisfy the rules of the kindergarten; the kindergarten must or should satisfy the needs of each individual child. If after all our attempts, the child is not happy there, it might mean that his socialization is not advanced enough and that we should postpone his going to kindergarten. In some cases, a visit to the child psychologist might be advisable. And I'm talking about counseling for us, the parent...

If the kindergarten experience has been a positive and a happy one, the transition to the elementary school should be smooth and not too traumatic. The first grade program is very different from the playing atmosphere of the kindergarten. It's not only fun and games anymore. There is a program of subjects to learn and the freedom of movement in the classroom is restricted compared to the kindergarten. Everybody is assigned a place that will be the same every day for the year. The group is larger, the atmosphere is less relaxed. It looks less and less like a family, and more and more like a detention center ...*not to say a jail!* Instead of playing only, the child must now do compulsory tasks. He has just entered the working world! **He is 6 years old!!!**

> "*America's future will be determined by the home and the school. The child becomes largely what he is taught; hence we must watch what we teach, and how we live.*"
>
> Jane Addams

With the attitude:"...*it didn't kill us*," we help perpetuate often destructive methods and practices that are possibly harmful to our kids. My approach is totally the opposite. Because of the incalculable value of the human spirit, we cannot allow ourselves to be carefree and nonchalant towards the atmosphere and the treatment we submit a child to. It's not the business of the kindergarten or the school to decide what is good and what is not good for our child. But because we capitulated, we disengaged, because we have been subjugated by authorities, religious authorities, governmental and civil authorities, because we have been dumbed down in so many ways, we have become irresponsible to the point of letting the government decide for us in domains where we should never let them dictate what's good for us and for our children.

Governmental authorities tell the teachers how and what to teach, without consulting the parents and the education specialists that psychologists and teachers are. They are instead, relying on some public servant, suddenly promoted education minister, a job where knowledge of child psychology has little or no importance, it seems! The school system perfectly delivers what it was conceived for: indoctrination, conformism and systematic de-individualization of the child for the benefit of a smooth and quiet rolling of the industrial and socio-political machine!

> *"The whole educational and professional training system is a very elaborate filter, which just weeds out people who are too independent, and who think for themselves, and who don't know how to be submissive, and so on - because they're dysfunctional to the institutions."*

Noam Chomsky

7

Our school system

"My children are what matters to me. And at the end of the day, if they go to sleep happy, confident, and knowing with every fiber of their being that they are loved, valued, and respected, then I've done my job."

Jennifer McGrail, The path less taken.

Our schools fall short of letting our kids *"know with every fiber of their being that they are loved, valued, and respected..."* Some believe that it's not the job of the school to raise our children. And lots of the teachers, if not the vast majority, are agreeing with that. They will be fast to tell you that their job is to fill the kids' heads with the knowledge contained in the curriculum, *period!* To them, the content of the curriculum is the Holy Grail. Well, I beg to differ with that largely shared opinion among teachers. The content of the curriculum should be very pertinent for the kids, but is it?

Now the content of the curriculum has not been chosen by the people like it should in any democracy. It has been entirely chosen by people who had the government's and the big corporations' interests at heart but not those of our kids. The fact that the government chose the curriculum without consultation with the parents and the teachers is not the biggest part of the problem with the school system. *The colossal* *problem with the school system is the "modus operandi" of that system: the **coercion***

Let me take you on a detour to try and illustrate a point. Let's turn the clock back before the kindergarten age. You have a 10 month old baby who starts to grab on furniture to hoist him up. He does it many times a day. He's learning how to stand up. He's learning how to keep his balance while standing up. He's, by instinct and creativity, getting ready to walk. Any time now, he will start to walk. With a little encouragement on your part, he's going to let go of the furniture and take his first steps maybe a bit sooner than if you left him alone. Most parents see that event with pleasure and excitement. But even without your prodding, he will walk soon, if he is normal.

What do you think would happen if, not only you didn't encourage your baby to walk, but you would discourage him from walking by saying a loud:"*No!*" every time he tries to stand up? And to make sure he doesn't walk, you kept him in a playpen with, on the top of it, a roof too low to allow him to stand up straight and walk, and same thing with his crib. I will never know the answer to this hypothetical experiment, but I would guess that he would probably still learn how to walk, bent forward and gradually, he would probably develop a curvature of the spine.

Now if we would free him at age 3 or 4 and let him walk without restriction, he might gradually straighten up his posture and probably end up walking erected like a normal kid. I believe a pediatrician would warn against this crazy behavior and foresee possible troubles with the spine and hips for a long time and possibly for life. And psychologically, there would most likely be serious sequels. Now, where am I going with such a terrible scenario? Nobody would ever come up with such a barbarian thing to do to a kid! It's against nature; it's against human rights; it's inhumane!

Let's move a few years forward in time and observe a group of 6 year old kids playing in a school yard. It's their first day in school. Some are chatting with their friends while playing some kids' games, some are running around, jumping ropes etc.: all normal kids' activities. Lots of body movements and lots of energy being spent. There are also lots of interactions at the relationship level. And you can hear a hum of chatter, laughter, yelling: the noise of a normal crowd of kids.

Suddenly, a bell or a buzzer sound fills the air with a sense of urgency. *It's class time!* **Immediately,** they must stop all their games and chatter to get inside and go to their classroom. *And there, real life just stops*! We bolt you to a chair, in a designated place, aimed forward toward the front of the class, and,-Oh yeah!- in silence. And for six long periods each day, you have to listen to instructions from the teacher, to practice writing stuff, talk in front of others etc. It's time to learn the three Rs.

For the first three years of school, the program will consist mainly of mastering those three subjects without which you can't get an education ...*they say*. It's the prerequisite to learning anything. In order to pass grade three and achieve the mastering of the multiplication tables, you are required to use your memory constantly. If you followed the instructions from your teacher, you now can write and read at a third grade level, or you should. In reality, not everybody can master that feat. And if you have memorized your multiplication tables properly, you're up to snuff in math. By next September, you'll be in grade four.

Now we have grown accustomed to see kids from age 6 to age 17-18 spend 6 hours a day sitting in class. It's the norm, or... is it? For me, that questionable regimen is no more normal than keeping a toddler from standing up and walking! It's definitively not as radical, but if they were not forced to sit straight, facing forward and in silence, what is the chance that any of them would do it? And if any of them did it, we should be concerned. It's simply not a normal child's behaviour. Kids are meant to play; *not work!* I believe they can, through humanely designed types of play, learn anything they really need to learn.

Instead, the school regimen teaches them that it is normal to spend most of their days sitting and being told every move they have to do! Not only it preaches to them that it's ok to do so, but it forces them to do it! Is it only me, *or could there be a problem here?* Then, when we realize that 31.5% of them are fat or obese, we suddenly look down on them and preach to them that it's their fault that they are fat and to move their ass if they want to lose weight or at least not get fatter. ***And day long, we continue to force them to remain bolted to their seats!!!***

Until now, we have rewarded memory to the detriment of imagination, comprehension, judgment and intuition. I hope the class session as we know it, the conference type of class will give room to an experience that involves the students much more than the teacher. The teacher should be at the service of the students *and not the other way around.*

In her introduction to the Golden Notebook, Doris Lessing tells us that we should ideally say to every child during his school years, something like this:

> *"You are in the process of being indoctrinated. We have not yet evolved a system of education that is not a system of indoctrination." We are sorry, but it is the best we can do. What you are being taught here is an amalgam of current prejudice and the choices of this particular culture."*

When, like Doris Lessing, we warn our young generation that they are pushed into following a very well marked out path, used by our preceding generations and the present one, we have to make sure we do not encourage them to find a certain other path, different from the imposed one, where everybody will feel free and liberated. There is no such a path.

We must encourage them to find a path different from the imposed one, but also different from everybody else's. That is the principle of individuality and uniqueness of people.

Our school system, in 2014, is still trying to force students to memorize useless information they can access on their smart phone, or other gadgets in seconds, *if they ever **want** it or **need*** it.

The informatics era will completely upset the school system, especially at the secondary level. What will the teacher's job look like in another 5 to 10 years, I couldn't tell. I hope they will play the role of facilitators or guides and will help students in chosen and individualized curricula, where sports and arts will finally have the place they deserve. The last thing they should be is instructors/indoctrinators...

> *"The founding fathers in their wisdom decided that children were an unnatural strain on parents. So they provided jails called schools, equipped with torture called education."*

John Updike, *The Centaur.*

Our public school system comes across to most parents as that magic place that fills their kids' head with knowledge, their heart with the promise of a job after grade 12... *and happiness ever after!*

> *"You bolt any 6 year old kid, boy or girl to a desk and through 12 years of indoctrination and coercion, it delivers 80 % of them with a 12th grade certificate."*

Eighty percent with a 12th grade certificate is not bad. But:

> *"It also delivers 50% of them with the smoking habit, 40% with some drug addiction..."*

Anonymous

That's not so good... It would be interesting to see the results of a comparative study, but it's impossible. All kids that age from industrialized countries are also in school...How could we find out?

> *"Boredom is the root of all evil - the despairing refusal to be oneself."*

Soren Kierkegaard

8

Conditioning to control

"It will, of course, be understood that directly or indirectly, soon or late, every advance in the sciences of human nature will contribute to our success in controlling human nature and changing it to the advantage of the common weal."

EdwardThorndike

The powers that be need to control the populations in order to achieve the level of power they thirst for. And there are many ways to control people, some more efficient than others. One that appears to be very effective, if we look around us in our country and in the world, is the manipulation of beliefs or a systematic conditioning of the minds from a very young age. Condition a young generation properly and they will in turn condition their offspring and, in doing so, generations to come. The governments do it, the churches do it, school does it, and so do families, some more than others.

"When it comes to controlling human beings, there is no better instrument than lies. Because you see, humans live by beliefs. And beliefs can be manipulated. The power to manipulate beliefs is the only thing that counts."

Michael Ende

When people refuse to question their institutions, they are putting their kids' and their own welfare in danger. We should be skeptical when our destiny is in other people's hands, especially when we realize that lots of the people who are in posts of command are power hungry, egomaniacs, *when they're not plain sociopath.* Those are strong accusations and I'm aware of it.

> **"Education has failed in a very serious way to convey the most important lesson science can teach: skepticism."**
>
> David Suzuki

"If it sounds too good to be true, it usually is." Our school system, in spite of the good intentions of most teachers, does not deliver what it could or what it should. It has been created to condition the future citizen. A dumbed down population is much easier to control and predict. And, because it has been conditioned to believe what it's told, a dumbed down population, given the appropriate indoctrination, will do what it has been programmed to do in a high percentage of the cases.

You take the strongest living animal, you raise it from a year old with a chain in its leg, like a tether, attached to a post. As it grows, you diminish the size of the chain. After years, you trade the chain for a rope. A big rope at first and you gradually reduce the strength of the rope until you replace the smallest rope with a ribbon that the elephant could break and free itself without effort. What happen then? The elephant remains a prisoner of a symbolic tie. *It's a great illustration of conditioning!!!*

The same thing happens to us: being disempowered by our institutions using the most powerful and efficient tool of conditioning known as indoctrination. Breaking that ribbon, that tether, is a must if we want to give birth to ourselves and thus become who we're meant to be.

The remaining percentage of those who have not responded to the conditioning properly, will have to deal with the policing system of the country which will use convincing means -or coercion- to shut them up, if they dare express opinions different from the establishment's opinions. Let's get back to the school's star: the child.

9

The most difficult job in the world: raising children!

"The proper time to influence the character of a child is about a hundred years before he is born."

William Ralph Inge

The last thing I would try to do is to pretend that I know how to raise kids properly. I don't think too many people do. Lots of jobs in society come with a title, like Doctor, Lawyer, Accountant etc. Parent, somehow, doesn't call for a capital P! We bow in front of all these people like they are important. And they are. But what about Parent, the most important job there is? None of them has as important a job as a Parent. We can survive years without a doctor a lawyer or an accountant, but not a week without a Parent when we're a baby. And it's the less rewarding job on the planet, in spite of the fact that it's the most important job there is. And if we accept my humble opinion that most people don't know how to do a good job at child rearing, where do we turn for help?

At this point, I must clarify one thing. As you might have noticed on the cover of this book, I have a *Ph.D. ...in B.S.* That gives me the right to give my opinion on matters normally pertaining to the domain of psychology or sociology. And on that matter, Noam Chomsky gives us his opinion:

"If anybody thinks they should listen to me because I'm a professor at MIT, that's nonsense. You should decide whether something makes sense by its content, not by the letters after the name of the person who says it."

Everybody knows what a family is. The word comes from the Latin, *familia*, meaning *household*. A father, a mother and a child constitute a family. The family, as an institution, already begins to mark us towards the end of the gestation. The mother's vibrations and the vibrations surrounding the mother like those from the father, from the other children and from any person with whom the mother is in contact, all those influence the mother's vibrations and consequently those of the child to be.

However, the most important of all is the emotional state of the mother. If she is happy and peaceful, the child has all the chances on his side of being a calm and happy baby. On the other hand, if the mother feels some resentment towards the embryo, is unhappy and negative, that child might have a very worrisome start at life, to say the least!

At that stage, the child already reacts to music and to other stimuli like his mother's stress with its production of adrenaline or his mother's love for him with the production of endorphin which he feels through the uterine wall. We therefore start very early to react to the sensations coming from the outside world which are passed on by the mother to the child in formation that we are at that moment.

We must therefore plan the pregnancies in order not to expose the embryo to a toxic gestation on the part of a deceived or worse, of a mother angry for being pregnant. In that sense, I say that large families, in most cases, were the result of an ignorant if not malevolent religious tyranny, in the pursuit of a selfish and destructive agenda aiming at a greater number of catholic church members. In Quebec, that situation was very visible and its aim was double: to surpass in number the members of the protestant church and establish the predominance of the French language.

The mother's task is particularly primordial and complicated by the quality of the couple's relationship. In spite of being an exceptional mother, she will not achieve the desired results with her child's education if the couple's relationship is lame. Since there's neither perfect mother nor perfect couples' relationships, what should we do? Should we stop having kids?

We live in an imperfect world where all is relative. We cannot wait for perfect mothers in perfect relationships to continue having kids. One thing we can do, as a society, is to first grant reproduction more importance, to recognize the super important role that the mother plays in it and the wealth that children represent for the family and for society as a whole. The greatest miracle in the creation, for me, is the miracle of procreation. Until we understand that and grant to procreation the importance it deserves, we're crippling the process.

Soon after birth, we develop reactions to our environment. Brightness, darkness, noise, voices, colors, touch, all touches, pleasant touches and others, dry diaper, wet diaper, skin rashes, the warmth, the coldness, smooth surfaces, rough surfaces etc. The child absorbs everything. He is a human super sponge. But he is also a beautiful being rich in promises that we must help to grow with tenderness and love and with all the corporal and affective care required.

How can we make sure that the mother and the father will be good parents? We can't! It would be tempting to dump that responsibility on the ministry of the family. And we do it to a certain extent. For at least the first year, without hesitation, I say that the mother should stay close to her infant and that, for many reasons. First, it's very desirable that the mother breast feed her baby. Both benefit from breastfeeding in a lot of ways that are more and more recognized nowadays. And those benefits are long term both for the mother and the baby. If we accept this premise, it seems only natural and reasonable that the mother stay home with the infant for at least the first year, or bring the child with her at work whenever the work place is receptive to it.

It's part of the biological make-up of women and more so of mothers. After the first year, if she chooses to go back to work and she can't bring her child, the babysitting question should be pondered very carefully. Ideally, the mother should stay close to the child for the first 4 or 5 years. But the constraints of modern life render that option very difficult. Man on the other hand is not equipped to accomplish that task; either physically, socially or psychologically. He can be of assistance to the mother, and be active in the kid's life, but he will never replace the mother. The mother has a nurturing instinct and a connection to her child that man doesn't have and never will.

It just seems appalling to me that the school system would consider child rearing as less important than history or geography... Most of the subjects of the curriculum that we teach are a waste of time. In 2014, if you ask a 12 year old kid from an industrialized country what is the population of Titicaca and he can't give you the answer in 10 seconds flat, either he is really poor and doesn't have a Smartphone or a similar gadget ...or he is slow. Because most kids that age have gadgets that they know how to use and find anything they want to know ...*if they want to*! **It is not up to us to decide if and what they should be curious about!** *To temper with their curiosity is as serious as to temper with their DNA!*

Tempering with our kids faculties, like curiosity and the propensity to play is a lot like forcing a kid to continue to crawl when he starts pulling him up on furniture to learn how to stand and how to walk. To me, we do exactly the same thing when we bolt them, from age 6 to 17-18, to a desk for 6 hours a day listening to subjects they're not curious about or the least interested in.

We domesticate animals for our profit; *we shouldn't do it to our kids!* In the same manner, I do not agree with forced knowledge. To me it amounts to an intellectual rape. We can put food in front of people, and that's very nice. But we cannot force food -or anything else- on them! And we often do it figuratively to our children "*for their own good!*" We have inherited from previous generations, through culture mainly, a certain amount of know-how applying to most departments of life. Generation after generation that pseudo-knowledge gets crammed in people's heads willy-nilly.

So our parents repeated with us the methodology of child rearing their parents had used with them with a few exceptions or modifications learned mainly from reading or TV watching. Let's take breastfeeding as an example. Somehow, in a large part of the world, it was related to sex and had to be hidden at all cost. That prudish attitude was making it more difficult because of the secrecy surrounding it. It has become more accepted in public, but it's far from being the way it should be. Women are not welcome to breastfeed their infant in a store for example or on public transports. But in the last 20 years, some progress in that matter has been achieved in some part of the world. Let's hope one day it will not only be accepted, but strongly supported and encouraged.

Human beings are seldom stupid. They often act stupidly, but that doesn't always talk about them. Instead it talks about a process that has been applied to them and that is called indoctrination, cultural conditioning or brainwashing. It happened to them, it happened to us, it happened to our children, and it will happen to theirs. Does it mean that it's hopeless and that we can't do anything about it?

I certainly don't think so. I think we over raise our children. We force them to become the picture of what we believe to be the model of a normal child. We indoctrinate them with what we've been indoctrinated to a certain extent. In a way, we force them to become copies of us, like if what we are is the ideal way of being. And to achieve our goal, we often use coercion: blackmailing, bullying, and even physical violence. Our churches encourage parents not to spare the rod! The bible encourages physical abuse on our kids:

"Whoever spares the rod hates his son, but he who loves him is diligent to discipline him."

Proverbs 13:24

I guess, when we believe in violence, and in showing the kids who's the boss, any excuse is good, especially if it's sanctioned by the *"word of God."* Personally, I don't believe for a minute that God could be as mean as the bible depicts Him...or Her to be!

Pretty soon, your two year old notices that when he says *"No"* to your demands it bothers you to a certain degree. It upsets you. It disturbs you. From that observation, he realizes that he has just invented something new, and something very powerful. He can manipulate people in his surroundings. He can resist you, make you mad, cause your blood pressure to rise; in a word *he can piss you off!* And there's not much you can do to stop him, short of coercing him. He has just discovered power, and he knows how to use it and he has the firm intention to use it for as long as you will remain ignorant of child psychology, including that magic faculty called creativity.

And unless you learn fast how to encourage the explosion of creativity of that young two year old *"tyrant"*, you will have a serious problem that has just begun. In most cases, it's a phase that will last months or even years, depending on the manner in which you will react to this new incredible toy he has just discovered. Who doesn't like power!!!

So when you have a child, you should realize that it's a lifetime contract and it pays very well ...if you're good at it. A child is a very complex being that we must observe and study very carefully. It's fragile, mysterious and for years, totally dependent on others to survive. Of course the family, in 99% of the cases, assumes that function... or rather, *that privilege.*

The family does its best, but often wishes that the baby came with an instructions manual... It's very demanding and very worrisome at times. Every parent wants the very best for their child, but what is that very best? All your know-how in most cases comes from your upbringing and the prevalent culture. And you want your child to be civilized when he grows up and fit in society. Through indoctrination, he can be programmed easily to conform, which is the last thing parents should do. Therefore, his welfare is very threatened in most cases by parents full of good intentions...

How do we, as parents, threaten our child's welfare? From my personal experience, I would say in lots of ways. The first mistake we do as parents is to consider our kids as belonging to us, as being our property. And in doing so, we believe we have the right to shape them to fit the mold we have chosen for them. Why do parents choose to shape their kids a certain way? *Because they can and because they have been conditioned by their own parents, their school, their church, their peers and society as a whole to believe that it's in the best interest of the kids to do so.*

In 2013, in the news, we heard of an East Indian mother who, helped by an uncle, had her daughter killed because she married a poor rickshaw guy without the family's approval!!! Why would they do such an unnatural and unthinkable act? Because of the conditioning received through cultural indoctrination.

It is ill-educated, inhuman and inconceivable. But it was part of their everyday life. And, if she did it, I'm not sure that her maternal instinct was still operational after all the indoctrination and conditioning bombarded upon her by their culture which is predominantly religious and primitive to say the least...

And, talking about conditioning, I don't want to get ahead of myself and treat at length of discipline which I will do in more depth when talking about learning discipline in school. But let me say this. It's a department in which a lot of families go wrong.

> *"Punishment may make us obey the orders we are given, but at best it will only teach an obedience to authority, not a self-control which enhances our self-respect."*

> Bruno Bettelheim

If parents treated their kids the same way good dog owners treat their dogs, most children would turn out a lot better than they do at the moment. If we want good results with our pets, we never hit them. We always praise their positive behaviors and never put them down. We make sure not to lose patience with them and always treat them like we treat our best friends.

> *"Instead of yelling and spanking, which don't work anyway, I believe in finding creative ways to keep their attention - turning things into a game, for instance. And, when they do something good, positive reinforcement and praise."*

> Patricia Richardson

The third mistake of parents is preaching. Preaching doesn't work: at church, at home, in school or anywhere else for that matter. Preaching is an attempt at conditioning, which is an attempt at controlling others. In order to control their kids, a majority of parents use different methods. It includes: corporal punishments, bribing, threatening, blackmailing and many other destructive tactics of which is bullying. They learned it from their own upbringing, at home in most cases, and in school in all cases.

These are very serious accusations towards us and towards the majority of parents. Let me give you some examples of how bad most of us are at parenting. When we spank our kids, we are using violence and retribution. In doing so, we are teaching them that the use of violence is ok to make others conform to one's wishes. To those who do not agree that spanking is that bad, next time some friend of yours comes and visit with you, and does or says something you don't like, slap him on the hand with a frown on your face and see what happens... Either they will laugh thinking you're just kidding, or, realizing that you're serious, they will look at you with an expression meaning: *"You can't be serious! What's wrong with you? Do you realize what you just did? What's your problem?"*

Our child cannot formulate all these questions. And if he could, he wouldn't dare vocalize them! But he can and will be shocked and confused. He will be hurt physically and emotionally. He will be traumatized. We just dug a pothole on the road of his life's journey. And each time we talk to our kid while showing anger, we're telling him he is bad, and that we're temporarily withdrawing our love from him. How many more potholes do we plan him to go around on his journey to becoming who he really is?

> *"Punishment cannot heal spirits,(it) can only break them."*
>
> Barbara Deming

We do not have to have kids! In 2014, there are a lot of birth control devices allowing sex without reproduction. I think we have been desensitized to the extraordinary privilege of co-creating human beings. There's nothing on earth that gets close to that miracle we can make happen at will! We have to stop taking it for granted. One day, that great privilege could disappear overnight. A nuclear winter could make us all sterile for years to come and maybe forever. I believe we are acting very irresponsibly in the face of the miracle of reproduction. It's not there simply for our pleasure and glory! We do not own these children in the life of which we're mere temporary accessories! It comes with an enormous responsibility: helping them to become who they really are!

We have been raised by people who didn't have a clue about child rearing, not more than we did ourselves. How many more generations of children will have to be sacrificed before we wake up and shake ourselves out of lunacy? We're going through life dumbed down by our upbringing and the materiality of a life in which we run to stay ahead of the hands on the clock, of the traffic and of the street lights. We slave to please a boss, we run home to feed the family, we sit in front of the TV or of the computer for a diversion, we run to the store and spend more money than we earn, we stress under the load of debts we continue to accumulate, we put up with a few kids for whom we are not really accessible nor available.

My advice to all parents, including me, is this one: stop, look, listen! Let us stop the trepidation of our lifestyle. Let us look around us in nature and inside ourselves, where love resides.

Let us listen to our heart telling us the distress of our kids and of the society they inherited from us, which society is promising a very uncertain future.

With the aid of gadgets, they are putting up a wall between themselves and their peers and ultimately between themselves and others including you and me. On one hand, they are in relationship with maybe more people than we were, through texting, talking on their cell phones, on facebook and in a few other ways. We can often see them in groups, all in relation with others...*other than the people they're with!* How to explain that a person far away could be more interesting than the person next to you, which you chose to be with, in the first place? The phenomenon is too new for me to judge and condemn and to draw baseless conclusions. But personally, I look at that new phenomenon with curiosity and I somewhat worry.

On the other hand, I choose to keep a positive attitude. I cannot talk for you, but one thing is sure: they cannot be more dumbed down than I was at their age! Besides, in a few years, the gadgets of today will have evolved and God only knows what they're going to be. Let's remember that the past is gone, never to come back, thank God! The future is only a figment of our imagination that might never come to pass. *We only have the present.*

Now is the only opportunity there is to encourage in our children the growth of the seeds of curiosity, creativity, self-discovery, self-actualization, self-love and love of others and of the entire creation. What you see is what you get. This is it! We either pause, look around and inside ourselves, listen to our heart, and consider trying a new approach with our kids, or we will prolong the agony of a whole new generation. We could do worse than what we are doing at the moment; but we could surely do a lot better.

What good does it do to them to know that Krakatoa, is an island situated between the islands of Java and Sumatra in Indonesia, if they don't know how to take care of their new born infant? And here, allow me to get back to the first and most powerful school of all: the family. I call it the greatest school of all, because there's no other school that can do for you what family can do for a human being. Between birth and the age of 5 or 6, if the child doesn't receive certain elements essential to his physical, mental and spiritual development, there's no school that will be able to replace what that child is missing. He will most likely limp psychologically and socially, for the rest of his life, schooling or no schooling.

Because of the complexity of the job, as parents, we often create nearly insurmountable problems for our kids. *And probably more so if we refuse to question the degree of child rearing skills we possess.* We should approach the task of educating kids with great humility. The task is monumental. And we have in most cases received very little preparation other than what our parents have used on us with the little preparation they had received from their own parents... going back possibly millions of years.

What makes us believe that we know what we're doing? Because, *in reality, we don't!* But we don't like to hear that. Al Gore would say it's *"an inconvenient truth!"* But what if; what if that statement is true?

10

Kids and Creativity

"Human intelligence is much richer than we have been led to believe by industrial/academic education. Appreciating the full range and potential of human intelligence is vital for understanding the real nature of creativity."

Sir Ken Robinson, Out of Our Minds: Learning to be Creative

We often use the word creativity. What is it? One of the first manifestations of creativity shows up when the baby cries to get attention, physical and affective comforting like suckling at his mother's breast or, short of that, to get a bottle. Is a day old infant creative when he suckles at his mother's breast or is it purely the result of an animal instinct requiring no intelligence or thinking faculty on his part?

I do not believe him to be, at that level of development, more evolved than a month old kitten. Without the suckling instinct or reflex that he was already practicing in his mom's womb since the 6th or7th month, sucking his thumb, his fingers or his fist, he would need to be forced fed if we wanted him to survive.

By age 2, the child definitively shows some signs of creativity. When he answers *"no"* to your asking him to do something, his answer does not come from a reflex. If he answers or gestures no *to all of your questions or demands*, he is gargling with a new word he has just learned, very likely, and which he probably finds amusing. He is experimenting with a new sound. But if he says no when you offer him broccoli and yes when you offer him ice cream, he is demonstrating a capacity for reasoning leading to the acceptation of what he likes and to the rejection of what he doesn't. He is being selective, which requires a certain preceding experimentation and decision making ability, based on previous experiences and memory of the pleasurable ones, as much with food as with anything else. It's a clear example of creativity.

If we encourage the child creativity by using a non-coercive approach at all time, we might not increase his inherited creativity but we will allow him to explore his surroundings and to compose with the elements he finds in it. He doesn't need more creativity; he just needs to know and to feel that his creativity is a wonderful tool and that it is welcomed.

Before the renaissance, creativity was seen as a conduit for the divine. And during the renaissance, it was seen as coming from the abilities of "great men". Nowadays, what defines creativity and what is its connection to intelligence is still the object of a lot of different theories. Without consulting Freud, I believe that everybody knows what we're talking about when we mention creativity.

I believe it to be one of the most important faculties after the intelligence. From birth to death, we behave. Every behavior has creativity as an essential component. We choose all of our behaviors which will be positively or negatively creative.

"I think it's fair to say that personal computers have become the most empowering tool we've ever created. They're tools of communication, they're tools of creativity, and they can be shaped by their user."

Bill Gates

11

Curiosity, precursor to learning

"It is a miracle that curiosity survives formal education."

Albert Einstein

Our kids go to school. They have to. It's the law. And besides, *"how would they succeed in life without going to school?"* It is clear to all of us that I'm talking about the public school system. Let's assume for a moment that they would probably not succeed in life if they didn't get a school education.

I have a problem with that generally accepted notion. I do not agree that our kids get a good education in school. *I don't even agree that they get **any education** in school*. I believe that the result of their 10 or 12 years spent in school has at best, given them a certain amount of information and instructions. That was achieved through indoctrination, not to confound with education. Quite on the contrary, all indoctrination, be it from the school, the church or the TV is detrimental to anybody, adults and kids alike. It adulterates and dumbs down people.

Many times, through this book, I have been repeating that school dumbs down our kids without explaining how it does it. I will attempt to explain as clearly as possible why I stand behind such a controversial statement.

I believe curiosity to be the real motivation for learning. Not for learning just anything. But for learning *what we are curious about*. School presents our kids with a curriculum of subjects the government, 150 years ago, has arbitrarily chosen to satisfy their own expectations of what the kids should know, and be shaped like, to fit the establishment's agenda.

The governments of the time had thought that with the grades system, punishments,-often *corporal punishments*-and the promise of graduation at the end of grade 12 dangling over their head like a piñata, the trick was in the bag.

Well, as you know, it didn't quite work that way. Human beings are very resilient. Otherwise, people would get destroyed mentally and would cease to function as human beings. If on the other hand, we let the kids choose the real world questions that interest them and that they can investigate at leisure, we would be surprised by the results. In this last scenario, which has been tried, by the way, the teachers become guides and assistants to the students.

In an article from the web called: *"Does curiosity inspire learning?"* Susan Sherwood affirms that:

"this type of learning is deep, rich, meaningful and memorable to students. It not only teaches them content, it also helps them learn how to learn, to find sources, to assess data, to work cooperatively and to report findings."

Those are real world skills we hope to see in every one of our kids by the time they enter the workforce. That kind of learning experience is by far more enriching and more beneficial than what the conventional school system delivers... or tries to deliver. And she adds:

"This Allowing this classroom curiosity is difficult, time consuming and labor intensive, but it encourages and enables students to become lifelong learners, who will seek to satisfy their curiosity well beyond their school years."

In the present school system, we bore most students for most periods of the day for nearly ten months of the year, for at least the last 6 or 7 years of their schooling.

"Boredom is nothing but the experience of a paralysis of our productive powers."

Erich Fromm, The Sane Society

Have we ever studied the subject to find out what that paralysis of their productive powers does to our kids? When we talk about our productive powers isn't it synonymous with our creativity, our kids creativity allowed and encouraged to function unbridled, leading to some creation of their own?

Again and again, people tell me: *"I was bored in school and it didn't kill me. Why would it be different for them?"* I will attempt to give you a difference that I believe could possibly explain why they are probably more bored nowadays then we were then.

With the advent of the computer and all the electronic gadgets like the Blackberry, the iPhone and all *the "iToys"*, the young generation has grown surrounded by all that magical neuron-teasing technology. In comparison with those tools and toys, the teacher sounds like an old 14" black and white TV with only two channels: *dull and duller!* Guess who doesn't want any part of that chloroform TV programming?

Our kids, for the last 150 years have been forced to stick with that mental abuse for a period of 8 to 12 years of their precious formative years. And we are surprised when they turn to drugs! We should be surprised that they don't turn to murder!

12

Playing is serious business

"For a child, it is in the simplicity of play that the complexity of life is sorted like puzzle pieces joined together to make sense of the world."

L.R. Knost, Two Thousand Kisses a Day

I wish I had said those words...Wow! How powerful and beautiful! Let's look in the animal world and see what the role of play is. We have all had the opportunity to see kitten play together. It's like all they want to do is eat, sleep, poop and play...till they're pooped. Are they really playing?

I don't think so. I believe they are doing phys-ed, using gymnastics to develop their muscles and, in doing so, they enhance their agility and suppleness. They are at school, the school of cat's life. They are learning how to hunt, first, to feed themselves, how to fight if they can't avoid a conflict and how to survive. They are learning life and survival. How do I know that? I don't know that! *I believe that.*

Is it possible that nature or the cosmos or God has done so because it was the most natural way to learn...for kitten as well as for humans?

"Genius is play, and man's capacity for achieving genius is infinite, and many may achieve genius only through play."

William Saroyan

I tend to believe that we will never prove nature wrong. Kids, like kitten, like to play a lot. And I believe that until we find the way to incorporate learning of certain forms of knowledge inherent to their nature into their natural innate propensity to play, we're *"atrophying"* their creativity. We're tempering with their true nature and that has a very delaying impact on their becoming who they really are.

Am I kind of saying that we should put kids on a pedestal and worship them and handle them with kid gloves? I'm not. But it might give better results ...than oppressing them like it's currently done in the schools of the world. Let's suppose for an instant that the strong instinct or tendency to play for the most part of each day has nothing to do with playing and everything to do with learning.

I'm 100% in agreement with teaching: reading, (w)riting and (a)rithmetic to our kids. And the past shows that it's done in all industrialized countries and there doesn't seem to be a problem. Then, if it's not broken, why try to fix it? It's a good question and maybe it's perfect the way it is. Or is it? Is it possible that we could find a way of letting the kids roam free and play with their friends and still learn the three Rs without any constraint on our part?

"In an era of parental paranoia, lawsuit mania and testing frenzy, we are failing to inspire our children's curiosity, creativity, and imagination. We are denying them opportunities to tinker, discover, and explore - in short, to play."

Darell Hammond

Long before the advent of compulsory schooling, dog owners knew that if you want to teach tricks to your dog ...or educate him, you have to praise him often and reward him for his good moves. They knew never to hit them or scream at them. In doing so, you would have turned your dog into a nervous distrusting dog. Nowadays, most dog owners treat their dog like they treat their best friends. How is it then that people from 75% of advanced industrialized countries are still using corporal punishment in raising their kids? *Are our dogs more important to us than our kids?*

And consequently, how does 12 years of continuous schooling constraint on our children affect them? In spite of the widespread culture of corporal punishment, one fact remains. We don't know exactly what the sequels of such a questionable practice are. If it ruins the possibility of training a dog properly, is it possible that it's also fully contra-educational for kids?

> *"The creation of something new is not accomplished by the intellect but by the play instinct acting from inner necessity. The creative mind plays with the objects it loves."*

> Carl Jung

If we look back to our school years we should remember that the life of a student is seldom easy. In those long hours spent in school there were lots of terribly boring and sad moments that felt like an eternity. *Those units of precious time stolen from us were robbing us of our youth.*

13

Sculpting our own being

"Every block of stone has a statue inside it and it is the task of the sculptor to discover it."

Michelangelo

If you allow me to parody that quote I'd like to say:
"Every child has a beautiful creative artist inside of him and it is the privilege of parents and teachers to help it come out in full light for the world to see and grow."

With the help of a good teacher, or a loving adult, every child should learn to sculpt his true self out of his apparent self. I call it apparent self because the face we show to the world, often, is only the façade we believe is expected from us. We are a lot different and a whole lot more than that façade.

When we indoctrinate kids through the culture, in the family, in school and in church, we mold our kids into a certain type of person. And this molding into a certain type of person, the same for everybody, is very detrimental to individuality and uniqueness. And unless we treat our kids as individuals, their chance of becoming who they really are is greatly compromised. And short of being who they really are, they are condemned to a life of pretending to be themselves. They are who we told them to be and mold them into being.

And what if what we told them to be is an exemplary citizen? Anything short of being oneself is a waste of a life that we will have to come back and relive the right way the next time around. It's a waste of a life that could have been a celebration of who we really are. Anything else is just a sad parody of the greatest achievement of human beings: self-actualization.

> *"If education is always to be conceived along the same antiquated lines of a mere transmission of knowledge, there is little to be hoped from it in the bettering of man's future."*

> Maria Montessori

We all know the implication and strong influence of Maria Montessori in education with her private schools. And she went on to say*:*

> *"For what is the use of transmitting knowledge if the individual's total development lags behind?"*

We are not on earth first to become knowledgeable, or rich, or important. We already are all of these things. We're knowledgeable at the subconscious level. We're rich of the true wealth from our human nature. We're very important to self and to everybody else we love and who love us.

In order to achieve the sculpture of who we really are, we must remove from the block of personality, in which we have been "straight jacketed" by the influence of our milieu, everything that is not who we really are and remove from our path, everything that stands in the way of who we're to become. And among the things that stand in our way is the pressure from the ambient culture that compresses us to make us fit in that cultural pattern we call society through indoctrination and conditioning.

Most people think that if you fit in society, your parents, your teachers and the church have succeeded in raising you properly. At the risk of passing for an objectivist, I'll have to say this: far from being a sign of success, fitting something as screwed up as our society, is a sign of having capitulated and having resigned oneself to follow the herd of sheep on its way to jumping off a cliff.

In the same manner as the statue is already in the block of stone, the true nature and the self of the child are already contained in the block of the human being he is at birth. With the help of a certain type of adults with the proper skills and attitude necessary to guide a child in the sculpture of self, that child will sculpt the best rendition of the symphony that he truly is inside.

And that certain type of adults often comes under the disguise of a mother, a father, a teacher, a coach, a friend and any person overflowing with love. All the circumstances and appearances of these adults will vary in the infinite. But they will always share a common factor: respect of self and of others. And Respect never travels alone; its travel companion is Love. You can't have one without the other!

Ask the dove . . .

One day, curious, I asked the beautiful white dove,
The coveted secret from cradle to the grave,
That impregnates your life, with an eternal love,
And that gives its color for you to love and crave.

The discreet charming dove cooed very tenderly,
Arranged her plumage, flattered by my request:
"Answer to the enigma haunting you constantly,
Can't be found in science nor in scientist's quest!

Go question the swallow, the sparrow, the blue jay,
Where they get energy, their good mood, their singing?
Get down low, if you please, look at the rose, you may.
Its grace and its color, and its divine smelling.

To the kitten, the cub, the entire nature,
What is the ingredient of their great alertness,
Mystery that haunts you, and intrigues and tortures.
The dolphin, the otter, their plays their foolishness,

And all, in their language, their murmur, their twitter,
Their wing span, their soaring, you must believe me, Man,
Will give you a drawing, an image, a picture,
Made of plants and of birds, animals and humans.

Put your hands in the earth, from inside from outside,
Your head up in the clouds, your face in the flowers,
Renew your connection with the cosmos, don't hide,
Re-attach missing link; give the heart its power!

Then you will understand, not with your head alone,
Like those pseudo scholars, but from inside your heart,
Like children always do, in more ways than one,
Cause Love is everywhere, for all on this good Earth!"

Demande à la colombe, Roméo Gauvreau, Jan.2000, English
translation May 2013

14

Self- esteem+self-love =Happiness.

"There is overwhelming evidence that the higher the level of self-esteem, the more likely one will be to treat others with respect, kindness, and generosity."

Nathaniel Branden

There is a tendency on the part of society to encourage our kids to emulate some models like teachers or war heroes etc. For some reason, I've always been against that practice. When I was teaching, I would sometimes tell the kids: *"It's good for me to be me, but not for you to emulate me, to choose me as a model. Becoming who you really are; there's your model to emulate and the only true one."*

If by any chance I do something that you admire, or treat you in a way that makes you feel good, do it unto others.

"I do not feel that we should set up people as "models"; rather actions, thoughts, principles."

Noam Chomsky

To look up to somebody and try to become like that somebody detracts from trying to become oneself. To imitate somebody postpones and sabotages self-actualization. In the whole of the creation, there's nobody like you or better than you.

The word happiness must be one of the most flexible and polyvalent word of the English language. Most people know what it means and how it feels to be happy. When we experience it in the present, our conception of happiness is often real. It's when we dream of something that we often err in describing the acquisition of a material thing as a promise of happiness. A good example is people buying lotto tickets and dreaming out loud: *"I'd be happy if I'd win the lotto!"* Are people winning the lotto happy ever after? And talking of lotto, most people think the same thing when they get married... There are a number of states of mind we call happiness that are not really defining it. What does, then, define happiness?

On Thesaurus.com, Sonja Lyubomirsky concludes in her book *"The How of Happiness"*, that

> *"50 percent of a given human's happiness level is genetically determined (based on twin studies), 10 percent is affected by life circumstances and situation, and a remaining 40 percent of happiness is subject to self-control."*

There are many prerequisites for happiness besides self-control. I think that total health, mental, physical, and spiritual, is one of the most important factors in the equation of human happiness. Without that total health, the quality of life is seriously compromised. But, what comes first? Is health a prerequisite to happiness or is health a resultant of happiness? I believe it's possible for some people to be happy in spite of bad health, physical health, that is. I don't see it possible in the case of bad mental health. It's very difficult if not impossible for a schizophrenic or a depressed person to feel happy while in that state, or in spite of that state. But there again, *my Ph.D. is in B.S...* not in psychology.

Let's assume for a moment that we have the basics for survival and a minimum level of comfort. Let's also assume that we are healthy. What, then, is the next most important requisite for happiness? Without knowing in what order they appear, I would list these as primordial even if they do not, by themselves, procure happiness. Without air to breathe and food to eat, we can't survive. With proper shelter and clothing to protect us from the elements, we enjoy a kind of comfort in our life that is a big part of happiness.

Three quarter of the world population benefits from these basic needs, but only a certain percentage of them declare themselves as being happy. It is nearly impossible to be happy without having these basic needs met. We called these the strict necessities of life. It's one of those things that many only appreciate when suddenly it goes missing. Until then, we take it for granted and discount it as a reason to be happy about. The company of people is another one of these things we take for granted. There are people around us all the time and, too often, we don't consider that as an essential part of our happiness. But the need to love and to belong is one of our 5 basic needs, described by Dr Glasser in Choice Theory.

So if you go on a solitary excursion for months in the wilderness, in most cases, it won't take long before you miss the company of people. First and foremost we are social animals. And I could come up with a lot more contributing factors to happiness. What are some of the factors without which life becomes very difficult?

If we believe Sonja Lyubomirsky when she says that

"...40 percent of happiness is subject to self-control", we must realize that we *can choose* happiness as Dr. William Glasser puts it.

Without a doubt, freedom is a very important one of these factors. We take it for granted until we lose it or part of it. The first example that comes to mind is being sent to jail. In most cases, it's pretty difficult to be happy in jail. You lose your mobility freedom, your freedom of association, the possibility to fulfill your need for love and belonging and a lot more privileges we take for granted in society. However, among the restricted amount of freedom still accessible while in jail, is the freedom of attitude. You can choose to keep a positive mental attitude and do the best you can in the circumstances to keep as much sanity and happiness as possible. You should certainly take advantage of your free time to reflect on why you're in jail and ...on how not to get back in there, once out!

How do these notions apply to school and to our kids? Let's establish that most of our kids have all the essentials like food, shelter, clothing etc. which, in most industrialized country, they generally do. So can we say that our school kids are happy? There's definitely not a one-fit-all answer. Some are happy, at different degrees, and some are unhappy at different degrees. What is the role, then, of school in our kids' happiness or lack of it?

Since they're in school for about eight and a half months of the year, the drain on their happiness is pretty significant. The kids who are not happy before entering school, will probably become even less happy when they enter school. If they were not happy before entering school, it's for reasons that would be difficult to pinpoint. But let's look at a few of the most common of these reasons.

Let's say that Little Johnny is particularly shy. Facing his class every day is uncomfortable for him. The school didn't create his shyness, but it exacerbates it to a difficult level for him. Therefore he hates school and we can understand why.

Little Susie on the other hand is overweight and gets picked on and bullied. She really resent school and gets very depressed at times which compound her inactivity and eating habits problem. There again, her problem has not always been created by school, but can definitively get amplified by it. She often wished she was dead. What can the school do about these two cases of kid unhappiness?

As for Little Johnny and his shyness, the school system cannot do very much more than hope that, with time, he will get over his shyness. It should be particularly careful in not trying to force him out of shyness by forcing him to read aloud in front of the class or by putting him on the spot in any way. That would be very insensitive and cruel! His problem most likely comes from his reaction to his family upbringing. Shyness is often accompanied by a lack of self-esteem. The family and the school, both, should get every opportunity to give tasks to the shy kid at which he has a great chance of succeeding and praise him for his effort, whatever the results. For every ounce of confidence and self-esteem you gain, you lose a pound of self-loathing and self-doubt.

> *"Confidence is a life ingredient that is essential to success and wholeness. It is perhaps the single most important trait that enables seemingly average people to do and become all that they can."*
>
> Steve Goodier

If I had to choose the condition *"sine qua non"* of happiness, I would say: self-love. But to have self-love, you need self-esteem. And to get self-esteem there's a prerequisite. You get it mostly from enjoying unconditional love from parents who love themselves unconditionally. And if you have that gift of love, you can conquer anything else. The sky is the limit! If you don't have that precious gift in your life, everything else will be out of focus and you will manage through life limping severely in most cases. With determination and patience, some of you, in time, will have the opportunity to parent themselves the right way, this time around, and regain self-confidence and self-esteem. A good self-esteem and self-love go hand in hand and; together, they pave the road to happiness.

That is what Sonja Lyubomirsky is alluding to when she says that *"40 percent of happiness is subject to self-control."* Otherwise, there would be no hope of happiness for a large part of the population who got neither unconditional love at home or at school. And without that unconditional love, it is difficult for the individual to develop a feeling of self-worth.

Nathaniel Branden, in Psychology of Self-Esteem describes self-esteem as *"the integrated sum of self-confidence and self-respect",* which he describes respectively as *"a sense of personal efficacy and a sense of personal worth."*

The school should try to put in place an atmosphere of play where every child feels self-confidence and self-respect. To feel confident, you have to be in a game in which you win more often than not. Loosing repeatedly at a game you haven't chosen, and that you don't like, will only contribute to boredom, frustration and the irrigation of self-confidence. It might not destroy your self-esteem, but it's certainly not conducive to building it.

To somebody who asked me why I quit teaching in 1972, I remember answering that I felt as an accomplice of a systematic deformation of our youth. That person looked at me funny and probably felt sorry for my misunderstanding of the great opportunity that school represents for our kids.

The school system has gotten away with religious, political, and psychological indoctrination for centuries because nobody dared to stand-up to them and risk his or her reputation until very recently. Big systems like the church, the government and the school are big monuments to tackle. Until the people stand up and demand changes, they'll continue their reign of deception and abuse at the expense of the whole society, but particularly our kids. And all three of them operate with the same method: conditioning through indoctrination. In other words: manipulation of the psyche through systematic brainwashing.

Every kid hungers for love, justice, respect and the opportunity to learn. In other words: for self-actualization. Always, they hunger for unconditional love which a percentage gets from their parents, but in our schools, they seldom get it. And there's no knowledge more important than knowing and feeling that they are loved by those who choose the mission of co-parenting them and of helping them learn how to learn and how to become who they really are!

I would say that for a large majority of students school is more a torture than a pleasure. From some study I read, 70% of girls and 80% of boys only like it some, compare to respectively 30 and 20% who like it a lot.

"In a universe where all life is in movement, where every fact seen in perspective is totally engaging, we impose stillness on lively young bodies, distort reality to dullness, make action drudgery."

Marjorie Spock

Let's think outside the box for a moment. Suppose your kid is one of the 30 % or 20 % who likes school a lot. You're a lucky parent and they are lucky kids; a lot less friction for you both. That's one way of looking at it. If you are one of these lucky parents, you might not agree with what I'm going to say next.

I believe your kid's future happiness is in jeopardy. *It's not normal for a kid to like school a lot.* School is an abnormal system that forces kids into accepting coercion as being good for them. Coercion is not good for them, or you or me or for anybody for that matter. Some advance the reasoning that coercion is at every level of society. They are right. Therefore, we better prepare our kids to be able to cope with and survive in spite of coercion. In other words, we want them to fit in society.

I can understand that reasoning, but I can't share it. Most people agree that our civilization is not healthy; there are too many kids starving in the world, there's global warming, racism, wars, subjugation of women in more than half of the world, coercion at all levels of society in every country and a lot more sufferings that could be avoided. I can already imagine people calling me an idealist and a utopian.

I do not believe for a minute that we could bring about a perfect world in a million years. But I believe that it's part of our human challenge to try and improve the world we have inherited at birth. Between a perfect world and the world of 2014, there's lot of room for improvement. And the best example I can think of, is the contribution of W. Edwards Deming with the creation of *"lead management"* and of William Glasser with his implementation of non coercive *"Quality Schools"*.

The workers from a *lead management* workplace will be more aware of the coercion in society and will not contribute to it at home or within their circle. Same thing happens with the kids from the *"Quality Schools"*. They have a much more normal life, are happier at school and at home and mature faster.

15

Self-actualization

"Human beings are not born once and for all on the day their mothers give birth to them, but... life obliges them over and over again to give birth to themselves."

Gabriel García Márquez

Kurt Goldstein defines self-actualization as: *"the tendency to actualize, as much as possible, [the organism's] individual capacities"* in the world. The tendency toward self-actualization is *"the only drive by which the life of an organism is determined."*

If we apply this definition of self-actualization to our kids, we must realize the enormous responsibility for us parents not to dwarf our kids' evolution in an effort to shape them and mold them to fit the present culture. Like for a plant, let's say a rose bush, we must provide all the necessary elements required for their growth, like love, life necessities and guidance, but we must avoid to expect our red rose bushes to produce yellow roses. It can be done through grafting, but we should reserve that procedure for our plants, not for our kids.

I will use a rose bush as an example to illustrate Mr. Goldstein's theory. If you ever observe a rose bush in your garden, the plant is very generous and bears flowers the very first year, in most cases. If that plant doesn't get trampled on or crushed by the accumulation of snow, given a normal mixture of sun and rain during the season, it will very likely produce an abundance of flowers in the subsequent years. We appreciate the plant mainly for its flowers and their nice aroma, but the bush itself is quite beautiful.

As you can see, there's more to the rose bush that meets the eyes. The beauty of its flower is what gets our attention first, then its fragrance mesmerizes us, and the beauty of the well furnished bush completes the scenery. Throughout that whole process, except during winter when it's dormant, the rose bush never stops its evolution. During spring, after the cold weather and the frost in some areas, it undertakes the task of redecorating its branches with leaves and buds to offer us another season performance. Year after year, for decades, it will never forget to intoxicate us with its fragrance and to astonish us with its beautiful symbol of love.

> "... *life obliges them over and over again to give birth to themselves*."

Like Gabriel Garcia Marquez tells us, *"birth is just a step in the evolution of a human being"*, a point in time in the sculpture of a beautiful and sophisticated piece of art that will never be completed however long we live. Like those rose bushes, season after season and life after life, we come back to accomplish ourselves and the creation. In the language of the rose we are perennial. In ours, we're eternal!

Finally, for Mr. Goldstein,

> "...*at any moment the organism has the fundamental tendency to actualize all its capacities, its whole potential, as it is present in exactly that moment in exactly that situation in contact with the world under the given circumstances.*"

16

The P.R. factor

"Every relationship is illusory, but we can't do without others. The external world continuously provides you with the opportunity to see and to observe yourself, and thus gives you a chance to transform yourself." (Author's translation)

Swami Prajñanpada

We are constantly in relationship with something or somebody. In the same manner as we are constantly making choices, from birth to death, every minute of every day. Dr William Glasser advances that theory in "Choice Theory", one of the most important books he ever wrote, I believe. In the last 6 years, after taking basic training courses in Reality Therapy and Choice Theory, in short, RC and CT, from the William Glasser Institute with Lucy Scott as coach, I totally believe his theory.

As for what I call the P.R. factor, it means the personal relationship factor. We are totally immersed in relationships. We were born because of a combination of many types of relationships. Our parents first had a social relationship with each other, a romantic relationship, a loving relationship, a couple's relationship, all of which brought them to a sexual relationship and finally a loving nurturing relationship towards each and every one of us. And since then, we never stopped relating to ourselves, to others and to everything else in our surrounding world.

I believe that a comprehensive study of human relationships and of their critical importance in the pursuit of life's success and happiness is primordial. We must try to help students understand the importance of being able to establish a good relationship with their parents, their friends, their peers, all people with whom they share a part of each day, at school or during their free time. The relationship to oneself is of utmost importance if they want to come to know themselves, to accept themselves, to love themselves and also to forgive themselves. One must be able to love oneself before being able to establish satisfying and happy relationships with others. And how do we teach that to students?

We don't; not really. Not the way school understands by teaching. The best way, I believe, is by being ourselves with them and by allowing them to be themselves with us. If we don't alienate them in the first place by our coercive attitude leading to indoctrination and conditioning, relating to self and to others will come to them naturally with the normal apprenticeship of life. The first of the five basic needs of all human beings is survival. The other four needs are psychological needs and the first one of these four is love and belonging. If we have problems concerning relationship with self and consequently with others, we will have serious problems with love and belonging. And if we cannot give and receive love, we'll wither like a plant without food, water and sunlight.

That capacity to relate to self and others in a satisfactory way is one of the most essential assets in life. Without it, life will be non-productive and miserable. One of the problems that having good relationships with self and others would help curb is bullying. It would have a far better chance at succeeding than coercion. Coercion never worked and never will. Love, respect and understanding are the principal means of education and of a successful social life in general.

We should concern ourselves with the school as a system and its influence on children. Personally, I don't believe that it respects these young human beings upon which it applies too much constraint. It's an intellectual and moral prison and we know what jail does to human beings. Until we understand that, and respect these young people and treat them like we treat our best friends, school will continue to be a dumbing down factory!

And instead of looking at drop-outs like they're failures and losers, ask them why they did it. They will tell you that they could no longer take the abuse from that system and from a large number of teachers who disrespect and even bully them on a regular basis. But that, you will not hear if you are a teacher using constraint; they're scared of you and of what you might do to them.

Oh! They'll also tell you that school is stupid...and I happen to agree! To me, their dropping out is a sign of resisting the erratic and abusive regime of the concentration camp we call school and the twisted conditioning we call education. We should therefore hire teachers not by what they know *but by who, what, and how they are.* Instructors are many, *but real teachers are few...*

We have to keep in mind that for 12 years of their formative years, our kids have experienced a false mini-society in which the relationships were not normal. First the relationship to the teacher was one of boss/employee or king/peasant. That type of relationship is common in our culture: boss/employee at work and government/citizen in society. Those are not healthy relationships.

There is a philosophical debate about what should be considered normal. But I won't stray from my beaten path. Let me say this. If the kids wouldn't be in school, they would more likely be at home with a parent, whenever possible, at play or at work; all normal situations. In this scenario, they would not normally be coerced every day for 6-7 hours a day. In the best families, they would not experience coercion but cohesion, cooperation and respect. In the average family, they would experience some coercion some time; not all of the time like in school. Just sitting at your desk, if you don't want to be there is a form of coercion on the part of the school...and of the parents.

It must have been in the spring of 67, when one day, in a *"Personality"* class,—one of the classes the school was looking at as a useless time-filling subject—I took 45 minutes to try and explain to my grade 11 students the importance of learning how to create and maintain a satisfactory relationship with oneself, first, and then with others. I can still visualize Line, my niece, sitting in the front row, with, on her face, an expression of somebody seeing a ghost. Everybody was so serious that we could have heard *a fly walking on the ceiling*... I was the only one disturbing the silence... And their silence was strikingly impressive! They were listening with a degree of intensity and curiosity rarely seen in class. I had added in conclusion:

"If you do not learn how to establish and maintain a good relationship with yourself first and then with others, you are going to waste your life away!"

What a pleasure it was for me to read a similar statement in one of William Glasser's books 40 years later!

17

Homework

"Homework allows students to practice the skills they learn during school. This helps the student retain the knowledge gained during the day rather than school being a pointless waste of time because nothing was learned or remembered."

Anonymous

To tell the truth, I'm not sure of the percentage of parents who are in favor of homework for their kids. The spectrum goes from being fanatical about it to being completely opposed to it. I understand the argument of the parents who believe that their kids acquire knowledge and receive an education in school. I understand them, but I do not agree with them believing that their kids inherit knowledge and education in school.

In my conception, education, in school, can only be achieved after a respectful relationship or genuine connection has been established between the two parties involved. An education cannot be given or imposed on a student, via coercion or any other means. That's not called education; it's called instruction, indoctrination. And indoctrination is never a positive experience. Instead, it dumbs down people.

The information received through indoctrination does not constitute what I call knowledge. Other than through physical education, sports and extracurricular activities, I firmly sustain that from grade 6 to grade 12 included, our kids acquire hardly any knowledge or education in school. At the head of this chapter, I reproduced the quote of a parent expressing his favorable views of the homework practice. I will now share with you the opinion of a student that reflects what a great majority of students think of homework.

> *"Students are already kept at school for 7 hours straight, now you're going to take even MORE time away from us when we're at home? ...leaving us no time to do things that we actually want to do. There's no time to spend with family."*

> Anonymous

I do not believe for a moment that teenagers hate homework, *first*, because they want to spend more time with their family. In America, nowadays, kids want more time to play games, to spend time with their friends and communicating on their electronic gadgets. I do not blame them for using that new modern escape from the stress of their school lives. Their lives are boring, wasteful, and senseless and in their words: "It sucks!" Boredom is very difficult to cope with for anybody. I see it as a kind of mental torture that impedes the child's self-actualization. And school forces them into the worst boredom they'll ever have to endure.

I believe that boredom is a situation in which your need to play, your curiosity, your creativity, your desire to learn and have fun are all of a sudden and all at the same time compromised by the school agenda, in order to condition you more successfully. And that happens, for 6-7 hours a day, 5 days a week, plus homework week nights and weekends. In my view, homework is useless, insensitive and plainly irresponsible. It's a dinosaur from the19th century way of thinking that we should relegate to the museum ...with the other ones! It's an inhumane practice and it should definitively be abolished.

ROMÉO GAUVREAU, B.A., PH.D.,...IN B.S.

"If children are not required to learn useless and meaningless things, homework is entirely unnecessary for the learning of common school subjects."

Passage from *Parents magazine*

18

Discipline

"To focus on discipline is to ignore the real problem: We will never be able to get students (or anyone else) to be in good order if, day after day, we try to force them to do what they do not find satisfying."

William Glasser, Control Theory in the Classroom

One complaint we hear more and more is about the young generation and their lack of discipline. They exercise less, stay up too late, spend too much time on their gadgets, gaming, talking or texting their friends. Lots of them abuse alcohol and street drugs. Lots of the older generation sees it as a lack of discipline, and it possibly is.

Then comes the big question. Are the kids of today less disciplined than we were? If we consider abstaining from certain behaviors being disciplined we would tend to say that they are less disciplined than we were. And maybe they are. But If I didn't spent a lot of time on the phone, didn't eat much junk food, didn't drink alcohol or smoke pot, it had nothing to do with discipline. *It just was not available to us therefore we had no merit in abstaining.* On the other hand, we had access to junk food in the form of sweets like cookies and sugar. I was, and still am, addicted to it. We were addicted before we knew how to walk. I heard that some mothers were giving a bottle of warm water with sugar to their babies to help put them to sleep faster...

In the mentality of the days, being a drunk or an alcoholic was really frowned upon by most people. It was seen as a mortal sin and a dishonor to be an alcoholic or a drunk, and there were not many of them around or... it was very well hidden. As for street drugs, it just was not really accessible to people in our area before the sixties, as far as I knew. Around 1965, when I started teaching, I started hearing about some kids using pot and hashish. As far as big centers like Montreal, it could have started years earlier. But it was a taboo subject and it was kept very hush-hush.

There are also many types of discipline. The military discipline, which I find abusive and robotic, doesn't teach normal everyday life discipline. It has one objective and it's to form efficient killing machines. Too often, military trained people believe in imposing a military discipline at home to their children. It's very detrimental to their self-actualization and happiness.

There is the self chastising discipline which is masochistic and destructive. It's a form of ascetic discipline found in most religious groups. The celibacy of priests is the manifestation of such an unnatural life regimen which continues to be imposed on its priests by an archaic religion which everybody can identify. Going against nature is never beneficial, whatever the motive. It comes from a fanatical indoctrination and is a deviation from normalcy. (My next book, *"Catholic Religion: The most infamous deceit ever attributed to God,"* will leave no doubt about my thoughts concerning that *cult...)* In doing so, the individual detracts from his self-discovery and self-actualization. It compromises his progress in the pursuit of becoming truly who he really is. It's not discipline; it's self-castigation. Is it to say that discipline is detrimental to human beings?

Many types of discipline are, but none of them is true discipline. Instead, most of the time it's subjugation to coercion, voluntary in the case of the military discipline and involuntary in the case of school discipline. I believe it to be detrimental in both these cases.

What we conceive as discipline, is, most of the time, a line of conduct imposed on kids mainly by adults. That imposed line of conduct is not discipline. It's simply an honorable form of bullying. I say honorable because it's not only accepted by the government, the school authorities and the society in general, but even by most parents. Society has inherited a culture that has been manipulated to satisfy the interests of the Establishment.

In spite of that tendency of our culture to remain a puppet of the Establishment, there are some people who condemn that antiquated coercive way of thinking and who choose to believe in the resiliency of human beings and to a certain type of discipline that is recommended and essential for adults and kids alike.

> *"Right discipline consists, not in external compulsion, but in the habits of mind which lead spontaneously to desirable rather than undesirable activities."*
>
> BertrandRussell

We should try to teach kids to be very careful, if and when, using credit and its traps. That's a very important department of life that threatens peace of mind and financial stability. How can we help them in that department while they see *a great majority of adults buying impulsively what they want instead of what they need **and what they can afford?***

One of the ways to try and help with that epidemic problem would be of having some people who are in a very difficult financial situation come and talk with the students about their experience with impulse buying. It talks louder than theories and preaching, and it would be cathartic for both the students and the invited guest. Hearing the consequences of bad buying habits on people's peace of mind and all the fallouts on the partner and the family would be a possible eye opener for these *life* students. There again, I don't believe that, in itself, it would stop kids from wanting gadgets they can't afford. However, since it's not preaching or indoctrinating, it might help them realize how it feels to be indebted and its stressing consequences.

And here, I want to underline a point of importance, I believe. If the school kids do not learn how to use all the gadgets that we see them use any time they have a chance to do so, when they graduate from school they will be the worst kind of illiterate people the world has ever seen. In ten years, most of the present gadgets will have been replaced with faster, smarter, lighter and many other improvements, but furthermore, there will be a myriad of new gadgets for which there are no words yet. The gadgets of today and the mastering of them open the door and give access to the world's workforce of tomorrow. It's like the three R's of a time that is no more. It's a *"do or die"* challenge!

There's one thing we must try to understand: those gadgets are making obsolete the need for the knowledge we're trying to impose on them today all over the world. With the computer and these gadgets, they need hardly any of the knowledge we believe they need. They have the tools and the know-how to access any information they'll ever want or need.

We don't have to fill their jugs anymore. It was detrimental when we did it in the past, and it would be very insensitive to try and continue to do so. As teachers, we are there to help them learn how to learn. Allow them to live some experiences through which they will experiment life. Let's encourage the freed up mind to learn really valuable knowledge like the answers to these important questions: *who am I, who are you and how can I help you?*

The Greeks about 6000 years ago had an inscription in the temple of Delphi which was saying: *"Gnoti Seauton"*: *"Know thyself."* You cannot love yourself until you know yourself and you cannot love others until you love yourself. And to get to know yourself, you need a form of discipline which is paramount to one day knowing yourself. If you know everything else there is to know in the universe around you and you don't know yourself, you're a helpless confused soul on this magic journey we call life.

That form of discipline so important on this journey towards self and the other is multifaceted. The most important facet is to make the decision as young as possible to never lie to oneself knowingly. Lying to others is also to be avoided as much as possible until you have evolved enough to not need it anymore. This is of the utmost importance. One of the ways of lying to ourselves unknowingly is to accept any form of prostitution: subjugation to conditioning, to brainwashing and indoctrination. Indoctrination is always destructive even in the hypothetical event that the content of the indoctrination would be true, -like in religious indoctrination-which is never the case. Indoctrination is the most powerful tool for controlling people by manipulating their beliefs.

A good way of protecting self from outwardly control is to never accept any belief that doesn't pass your censure or your severe screening at the gate of your soul. Being skeptical of anything foreign to self seems to me like a condition *"sine qua none"* to achieving the *"gnoti seauton"*(know thyself!) of the very wise Greeks of eons ago. The amount of knowledge needed for the conduct of life other than the knowledge of self, is only as a tool to make life's journey easier, more comfortable and more enjoyable. It's also used for entertainment purpose, as a titillation of the cerebrum.

Discipline has different meaning for different people. And the only real meaning of the word discipline, for me, is a certain mental resolution of an individual in the pursuit of knowledge of self. This resolution is to choose to travel roads going toward the discovery of self and the other and no other roads, whatever the promises of reward at the end of those illusory roads...

> *"Punishment may make us obey the orders we are given, but at best it will only teach an obedience to authority, not a self-control which enhances our self-respect."*
>
> Bruno Bettelheim

Despite all its decorum and its pretention of nobility, school only teaches our kids to obey authority –any authority-and not a kind of self-respect that makes possible the choosing of the only paths leading to self-actualization.

19

Bullying and Cyberbullying.

"Bullying is killing our kids. Being different is killing our kids and the kids who are bullying are dying inside. We have to save our kids whether they are bullied or they are bullying. They are all in pain."

Cat Cora

I fail to see what right our society has to tell bullies to stop bullying! Really! Some parents do it. Some students do it to other students. Some teachers do it to some students and to other people including teachers. Our governments consistently coerce us. If you want an example of it, just join a protestation movement and assemble in the street and see how long it will take before the police comes up with a variety of very unpleasant methods to have you get back in your hole and shut up! During spring 2012 in Montreal, Quebec, we saw a perfect example of it.

The government having announced its intention of raising the university tuition fees, the students' union organized a protest and they gather in the street.

Then I ask myself the question: *"What harm would it do for the government to invite and meet their union representatives and discuss the students' concerns and the government financial situation?"* These were all university students, all smart kids. Why did they have to go and protest in the street in the first place? These are not criminals... Why not treat them with respect and dignity?

Through a meeting, they would have had the chance to debate their point of view with the government and possibly come to an agreement. Whatever the outcome of the meeting, they could have come out of it with their head held high and the principles of democracy would have been copiously reinforced.

Instead, the government passed the bill 78 which basically removed the right to protest from citizens. That law requires that all protestations must be preceded by an 8 hours warning to the city, be composed of no more than 50 people and that the exact location and itinerary of the protestation be given in advance and a few other emasculating rules like that. The governments in power treat us ...like we treat our kids in school: coercion, lack of respect, bullying and the rest... Back to school bullies and bullying.

Bullying is not a recent problem in schools. I personally experienced it as a witness and as a victim of it in college (seminary) from 1950 to 1957. I believe that there was a lot less of it then than since 2003 or so with the gradual apparition of the cyber gadgets. Bullying is probably as old as the world.

I believe men have bullied certain other men and *probably most women* since the beginning of time. Countries have bullied other countries and are still doing it as you read this book. One just has to watch the news at night to see and hear about wars, be it countries against countries or civil wars, tearing countries apart and decimating the populations like we have in Syria at the moment (over 150,000 deaths) and in Egypt to name a few.

Having said that, I am totally against bullying against countries, against women, or any citizen, bullies included. In school, among possible causes of bullying, we must consider the high level of boredom causing frustration and aggressiveness among certain students, more than among others. Students who are victim of coercion at home, on top of the constant coercion in school, are much more prone to bully others.

If we refer to Wikipedia, we find this definition of bullying.

"Bullying is the use of force, threat, or coercion to abuse, intimidate, or aggressively impose domination over others. Behaviors used to assert such domination can include verbal harassment or threat, physical assault or coercion, and such acts may be directed repeatedly towards particular targets."

Wikipedia

If we believe this part of the quote:"...*the use of force, threat, or coercion to abuse, intimidate, or aggressively impose domination over others,"* the coercive attitude of our school system is a form of bullying. The bullying phenomenon should stop us dead in our tracks! *It's a red flag society can't afford to ignore!*

We are witnessing a reaction to coercion that is extremely serious and distressing... I don't want to throw the book at those kids; *I want to take them aside and hug them!* I believe some of their parents, their school and society as a whole have let them down. Their reacting in that manner is a cry for help. They are drowning in the stormy seas of the all engulfing coercion. They need help! If we don't take the time to help them get their life back on track, they will probably waste their life away.

They should be pulled out of school and sent to a Montessori school or to a *"Quality School"* whenever and wherever possible. Counseling, for them and their parents is a must. The psychological damage inflicted to bullies and bullied by the school, in all cases, and by the parents, in most cases, contributing to change a kid into a bully, is not the kid's fault.

If nothing is done to help the child towards recovery, he's facing a life of unhappiness at work and possibly of spousal and child abuse. Besides, among adults, nobody likes a bully!

"By their mid-thirties, 60% of people who bullied in grades 6 through 9 have at least one criminal conviction. ...they are also more likely to carry

*weapons than non-bullies and may develop antisocial
personality disorder."*

(tweenparenting.about.comParentingTweens)

The chance that the school takes any responsibility for that
serious problem is just about nil. Their argument will probably
be that they treat everybody the same and only a few bad
apples turn out to be bullies. It's true, but that argument, at
best, is no more than a lame excuse and a refusal to question
the school's way of using coercion as a whip to control students.

Many parents will tell me that it's the school's fault only,
but I disagree with that statement. The school coercive system
without a doubt is to blame, but if the parent-child relationship
was healthy, the parents should have reacted as soon as the
problem started. Their reaction should have been to talk with
their child and with the school principal and with a psychologist
to find out why their kid bullies other kids and maybe his
siblings. And hopefully if the home education is part of the
problem, we should get some help to correct the attitude of one
or both parents. *I do not believe that school alone creates bullies
if these kids have unconditional love at home.*

*"There is a subconscious way of taking violence as
a way of expression, as a normality, and it has a lot of
effects in the youth in the way they absorb education
and what they hope to get out of life."*

Salma Hayek

Again, I'm no psychiatrist but here's what I think. Give
me 1000 kids who have been unconditionally loved and
respected, at home and at school, and I can't see any bullies
emerging from that scenario. If by a slim chance, there are
one or a few, I would recommend having them tested for
sociopathy by a psychologist. Otherwise I don't believe you'll
encounter any bullies. But sadly enough, the conditions of my

scenario-unconditional love, both at home and at school-do not exist in 99% of the cases.

> *"Kids aren't born to be bullies, they're taught to be bullies."* (Author's emphasis)

Matt Bomer

Having established that both the bully and the bullied are victims, victims of a coercive attitude they had no choice but to endure, we must not add to the bully's torment by treating him like a criminal. He is not a criminal, at least not yet! But a high percentage of the bullies will end up with a criminal record if the parents don't react on time and in the right manner.

> *"Being a bully also increases the odds of future run-ins with the law. By their mid-twenties, former bullies have more traffic violations and four times the rate of criminal behavior than their non-bullying peers."*

(tweenparenting.about.com)

Bullying has always existed. We find it at every level of society, including in some families, between parents, between parents and children, and between siblings. It's therefore not surprising to find it in school. Consequently, it's a good place to start to educate them on how to establish a satisfactory relationship with self and others and therefore develop a good self-esteem. But it can only happen if we also work at eliminating coercion at the source: in their family (80-90%) in their school (99%). I don't believe punishments or threats will help solve a problem that is gaining alarming proportions. In doing so, we only compound the problem.

Lately, we hear a lot about a new form of bullying that didn't exist when most of us were in school: the vicious and relentless *cyber bullying.* Instead of being exposed to bullying mainly during recesses and in between classes on school days, victims are now harassed 24/7 on cyber space. The victims have no respite and nowhere to hide. It's an alarming situation!

I believe that strict laws calling for stiff penalties will be passed to try and curb that new trend. *It's a waste of time and money!* **It will not stop the bullying!** Yes, we have to find these bullies ...and help them before some of their victims commit suicide in desperation. They both need serious help if we want them to have a chance at a normal productive life.

Here's a new bill attempting to deal mainly with bullying. Let see what it's like. On November 30, 2011, the **Ontario** Government introduced Bill 13, Accepting Schools Act, 2011 in the legislature.

New Anti-Bullying Laws Across Canada, Yosie Saint-Cyr

> *"The Act would amend the Education Act to create bullying awareness week in schools and provide instruction regarding issues of bullying and dealing with situations where bullying occurs."*

Saint-Cyr continues on, adding a very important component of the act:

> *"...and if there is a promise to protect and counsel victims and perpetrators, while threatening legal consequences, we should be better able to deal with bullying as it happens, and hopefully to prevent violence from escalating."*

Did I read that well?

> *"...while threatening legal consequences!!!"*

The big guns had to be brandished! How could it be otherwise? Governments breed coercion!

If, as I believe, coercion at home and/or at school creates bullies, it would amount to adding insult to injury. If the threat of expulsion doesn't deter the bullies and they end up getting expulsed, what happens to these kids then? Where do they go, what do they do? The parents want their kids in school even if only for the babysitting advantage of school...

There's nothing the courts, the school or the parents can do that will solve the problem except removing the source of the problem: coercion in school and/or at home. **Bullies are not the cause of the bullying problem.** They are a sample of the victims of systemic coercion, a category of victims who end up reacting that way, while trying to stay afloat emotionally.

According to Wikipedia, bullying is rampant between students and other students, and between some bullies and teachers. Some teachers bully other teachers and some teachers bully parents. Some office staffs bully teachers, students and parents. Some principals bully office staff, teachers, students and parents. We even find some parents that bully principals, office staff, teachers and their own children

I see but one solution and it will take a while before we see tangible results. Certain attitudes of some parents with their children will have to change. The spirit of teaching will have to change. The number one lesson to teach kids will have to be the respect of self and of others. And to make the learning of that lesson possible, everybody will have to join in the effort to respect themselves, others, and these kids, always, and wherever they are. In doing so, kids will learn to respect and love themselves. After that, everything is possible.

And as much as the pursuit of such a transformation might seem difficult to accomplish, there is no greater pursuit of truth than that one. When we reach that goal, we will see the flourishing of a true civilization possibly for the first time on earth. I'm aware that for certain people, I will come across as an idealist and a dreamer and that the pursuit of such a goal is a utopia. But nothing is further from the truth. *We overcame cannibalism, didn't we?*

That it would be difficult to accomplish such a change in the foundation of our society and that it might take a few generations is definitively realistic. You surely remember the title of chapter number 3: *"Raising children: the most difficult job in the world."* Nobody has ever said that man's evolution would be easy and rapid and that the results were guaranteed.

But in working together towards such a goal, we help kids and ourselves grow in the process. And that's a big part of why we're on this earth in the first place.

Another part of the equation of bullying is the victim or the bullied. He is part of the problem in some cases. He is often a person whose spirit has been broken, often at home, and somehow he attracts abuse to himself by his negative attitude showing his vulnerability. And when teased, he doesn't react in proper ways. He doesn't know how. He needs help before he himself starts bullying younger and smaller kids in a compensating or a reactive kind of way.

As for the people who could help him and the bully, let's hope that they will see the light and not attempt to control the bullying by bullying the bullies.

The situation will improve, in time, but first the social inertia has to be tackled in order to accomplish any change to our institutions. There would be a lot more to say about bullying. A whole book wouldn't be enough to cover the subject properly.

In the next chapter, I will talk about the poor depressed bullied students who, out of desperation, end up taking their lives ...or thinking about it.

> *"The culture of bullying includes daily activities and the way people relate to each other. A bullying culture emphasizes a win/lose way of thinking. It also encourages domination and aggression."*
>
> Parsons

20

Suicide agony.

"When people are suicidal, their thinking is paralyzed, their options appear spare or nonexistent, their mood is despairing, and hopelessness permeates their entire mental domain. ...and the present is painful beyond solace."

Kay Redfield Jamison, Night Falls Fast:
Understanding Suicide.

I will abstain from trying to talk about suicide in a shrink jargon. Being bipolar myself and having been suicidal for long periods in my life, I understand and I empathize with victims of bullying who consider or commit suicide. To be as realistic as possible, I will use my personal experience with suicide ideation.

"Until you've had depression I don't think you're qualified to talk about it."

Geoffrey Boycott

As for the bullied, he is in greater danger of ending up depressed or suicidal or both. It's very difficult, even for an adult, to make sense of life while depressed. It's impossible for a kid. Depression takes away from the person his *"joie de vivre"*, his energy, his appetite for anything, including sex and food. At that point, hope has disappeared and when hope goes, we all face the same feeling: we wish we would go to sleep for ever. We want to stop hurting, but the pain is in the thoughts, and the thoughts are painful, *terribly painful.* And the flow of thoughts cannot be stopped. If we don't go for help,-chemical help or other- we're in danger.

Accompanying those hurtful thoughts, those torturous thoughts, there's a new thought that has moved in our mind: the desire to not be alive! Wanting to not be alive and wanting to kill ourselves are two different things, at least at the beginning. For some, the possibility of killing oneself is like a last resort exit, a way out of the nightmare, an ending to the torture. But the thought of killing oneself is a very scary thought.

> *"It's often difficult for those who are lucky enough to have never experienced what true depression is to imagine a life of complete hopelessness, emptiness and fear."*
>
> Susan Polis Schutz

Finally, when you meet a depressed person, especially a kid, please have empathy for them. Their suffering is beyond description. Your telling them how to fix their depression *will only tell them that you don't understand.* A word of encouragement and understanding or preferably a heartfelt hug, is all one can do for them. They need love; *not advices...*

I wrote a poem on suicide ideation expressing my feelings face to such a scary attraction...

The Call from Thereafter

"Just a thought, an idea, a strong, tenacious thought,
I visit you often, though sporadically,
I hang around and stay, far too long, even though
Too often I scare you to Death, radically.

I'm the chauffeur for Death, the King, the supreme Host,
I have a vast audience, everybody knows me.
Even the fear of me, the way out and the ghost,
You see me as a threat, a con, cruel enemy.

If I come and visit, when you are calling Death,
I come to be of help, to end your misery.
You are always worried, about eternal debt,
For you, the pros and cons, you check so miserly!

You are really tempted, pounder my solution,
You sure are attracted, often fascinated
By the effectiveness of my resolution,
But the specter of Death leaves you alienated.

Nothing at my Master's compares with this torture,
This load you must carry like does a poor work ass,
Come with me, I promise, to soften departure,
And the relentless pain and poisons that harass.

Do not think about it, you must decide right now,
There's no hope of relief, you have to try something.
Do it now, do it fast, I know where, I know how,
Please, you must cease to fret, and hesitate and think.

Depression tortures you, future closes on you,
Nobody can help you, you're worthless anyway,
Nobody will miss you, like the thorns of the yew;
You're nothing, you're a freak, choose the time, choose the way!

These pills on your table, taken in quantity,
Would put an end to pain, without noise or trumpet,
You can do it right now, for your own enmity.
Just do it, do it now, no use to sweat or fret,

Then you will cross the door, and enter into bliss,
Where pain, hurt and sorrow make no sense anymore.
Come with me, I'm your friend; there's nothing you will miss.
So, be happy right now, forever, evermore..."

0-0-0-0-0-

The End, La fin, Al final, Ende, O final. Salut, Goodbye, Adios, Salute, Abschield, Aurevoir, Arrivederci, Farewell...

Rest in Peace, amigo!
Miss Sue

Roméo Gauvreau, the Fourth of Feb. 2013.

21

"He touched me and made me whole."

"We need 4 hugs a day for survival. We need 8 hugs a day for maintenance. We need 12 hugs a day for growth."

Virginia Satir

About a year ago, on the news, they were reporting about a measure a school board had put in place following a case of *alleged* sexual abuse against one of their teachers. And to prevent anything like that from happening again, they put a new rule in place saying that teachers were not allowed to touch a student anymore, even giving a hug.

If I remember well, even the kids in the school yard were not allowed to touch each other. I really start to believe that in order to occupy a post as a schoolboard member it helps to be narrow minded. It's appalling to find some people in roles of authority coming up with such drastic ideas. Who are these peoples??? What planet are they from??? Who were the sickos around that School Board table who agreed with -and voted for- such overkill measures?

If you google: "Teach But Don't Touch", you'll find more on that subject: *"Practical advice for school employees on avoiding false allegations of improper conduct with students."*

Everybody knows the gospel song: *"He touched me and made me whole"* by Elvis Presley. It's one of the trademarks of his career. Virginia Satir emphasizes the importance of being touched in her quote about needing 4,8,12 hugs a day for survival, maintenance and growth. It seems exaggerated, at first glance and I don't know of anybody receiving enough hugs (12) for growth. Most people, I believe, still grow emotionally, intellectually and spiritually, at different degrees.

Is it possible that we would grow a lot faster and reach a higher degree of self-actualization if we received our 12 hugs a day or so? I don't know the answer to that question, but I know one thing. When we hug somebody, we are giving that person a very important message. That message is multiple. It says or should say: *"I want you to know that I like you and that I want to connect with you. I want you to know that I love you."* That, for me, is the meaning of a hug, and in most cases, that's what it means. Most normal people accept, welcome and enjoy a hug. It's a much more personal and emotions filled gesture than a handshake. In that sense it's a spiritual ritual that might convey healing to both the giver and the receiver. It's a lot like holding hands. Instead, it's holding hearts.

Who is going to explain to me that we should discourage such a beautiful gesture? And instead of somehow establishing a connection between that and a deviant sexual conduct, shouldn't we instead hug our students more often, when the occasion is propitious to do so? Of course it has to be mutually desired. We can't force ourselves on someone that is not comfortable with receiving us.

"Hugging therapy is definitely a powerful way of healing. Research shows that hugging (and also laughter) is extremely effective at healing sickness, disease, loneliness, depression, anxiety and stress."

Marcus Julian Felicetti

Mr. Felicetti lists ten ways hugging benefits us of which I reproduced the first and the last one here.

1. *"The nurturing touch of a hug builds trust and a sense of safety. This helps with open and honest communication."*

One of the most important tools to reach happiness is to be able to connect with nature and people we live with. And in order to connect we need to be able to establish *"an open and honest communication."*

Considering how essential self-esteem is to our life's journey, we have to agree with the last of the ten ways hugging benefits us by boosting our self-esteem:

10. *"...From the time we're born our family's touch shows us that we're loved and special. The associations of self-worth and tactile sensations from our early years are still imbedded in our nervous system as adults."*

That hugs ***"connect us to our ability to self-love,"*** isn't there the most important part of self-actualization? If we have self-love, it's because we already acquired self-confidence, self-esteem, and self-respect. Isn't there the whole idea about education? What else do we get an education for?

Question:

Why doesn't the government impose on teachers at risk of deviant sexual conduct the lie detector type of psychological test determining if you have pedophile tendencies and which sex and what age group is attracting you towards deviant sexual conduct.

Such tests exist and the school won't use them probably because it's against human rights or some other stupid rule like that.

What about the human rights of these kids???

Parents, what about your rights and your kids' rights?

22

Holistic Education

"Education with a holistic perspective is concerned with the development of every person's intellectual, emotional, social, physical, artistic, creative and spiritual potentials."

(Wikipedia)

When I was still teaching, there were people I call *"academia nuts"* (fanatics of the academic subjects) who would have liked to see Phys-Ed disappear from the curriculum. For them, it was a waste of precious time that should have been used for learning, instead. What they weren't realizing was that physical education was maybe termed wrongly and that it was rather an important part of a total, holistic education.

What distinguishes holistic education *"...from other forms of education are its goals, its attention to experiential learning, and the significance that it places on relationships and primary human values within the learning environment."*

Robin Ann Ma

There's a lot more to Phys-Ed than what meets the eyes. When you execute a gymnastic prowess, you use more than your body muscles. Anytime you use your voluntary muscles in sport or gymnastic, you also use many of your mental faculties. In no particular order, you use your will power, your creativity, your agility, your body location perception in time and in space, your estimation of fear of danger versus real risk involved and through all that, self-confidence winning over self-doubts and reaching one more cog in the wheel of self-actualization.

To excel in gymnastics or in sports, you need to develop self-confidence, to manage your fears, to learn better movement coordination, to develop/increase team work aptitudes and character strength. You have to learn that what makes winners is not the final score on the score board, but how you played that game, your team spirit and that you had fun doing it. Anything else is but a lost game. To me, if you're a good sport and really good at team work, you have a great chance, first, to be successful when you get in the workforce, and, more importantly, to be successful in all your interactions with the people who are an integral part of your personal life.

Now, I'll establish a relation between Phys Ed and a potentially serious health problem. And I would not want it to shadow in importance what I just said about the benefits of P.E. I believe that physical education is more and more recognized as important since we have become aware of the overweight/obesity crisis in the population in general and among school kids in particular. In the last 30 years or so, our population weight problem has sky rocketed. "In 1979," according to The Obesity Prevention Source:

> *"14 percent of Canadian adults were obese. By 2008, 25 percent of adults were obese, and 62 percent were overweight or obese"*

(www.hsph.harvard.edu)

Among our school-age kids, the numbers are about half of the numbers among adults, but the situation remains alarming. Add the kids' new sedentary lifestyle, the access to junk food at nearly every street corner, when it's not in the school vending machines, add to that the frustrations of a coercive school system that abuse and bores them to death and you have a good idea of the problem's amplitude. That multi-faceted problem, I believe, will not be solved either easily or overnight. And the last thing we should do is to start blaming the parents or worst of all, the kids.

> Using World Health Organization standards of measurement, *"31.5 per cent of five- to 17-year-olds an estimated 1.6 million Canadians were classified as overweight (19.8 per cent) or obese (11.7 per cent) from 2009 to 2011."*
>
> (www.cbc.ca/m/touch/health/story/1.1154456)

I personally believe that lots of our kids are terribly discontented and frustrated with school and by extension, their life. The curriculum is less and less pertinent to their new lifestyle and therefore the teaching is more and more boring therefore more and more stressing. Teachers cannot compete or measure up to the electronic gadgetry. This type of school system was flawed from the beginning and I firmly believe that it won't last another 10 years. But we'll have the chance to talk more about it in further chapters.

Naturally, having as proper a nutrition at home as possible is a good step in the right direction, for kids and adults alike. Not only it's a more nutritive and less fattening diet, but at the same time it educates the kids on how to eat healthily. That's pretty well the consensus. However, we're only seeing the tip of the iceberg. It's only going to get worse because it's becoming more and more complicated to identify edible food.

The expression "junk food", we use to label fast food restaurants with, is now applicable to a large part of our grocery purchases. There's no such thing as a family with a good diet anymore. Some do better than others, but none have a good nutrition. *You read that well! I repeat:*

"There's no such thing as a family with a good nutrition anymore!"

How can I say such a thing? I'm sad to say it's the truth. There's a new phenomenon now in Canada, coming mostly from the U.S. that complicates the problem ten folds. The source of the problem is multiple and very complex. You heard about it, I'm sure, it's called GMO, or *"genetically modified organisms."* In the last 20 years that monster has brought a new dimension to the already complicated problem concerning proper nutrition. Genetically modified food is causing some changes in human DNA, the ramifications of which we haven't a clue about, other than making us fat or obese.

"Genetically modified foods are foods produced from organisms that have had specific changes introduced into their DNA using the methods of genetic engineering."

"(Wikipedia)

To that, add the problem of food processing, food enhancing and preserving with additives, plus the fertilizers and pesticides all of which are affecting what we eat in ways we're most of the time unaware of. Now, if we thought that food processing was bad, how about this GMO threat? And after we have been made aware of it, we remain ignorant of what food it has been done to. One of the very complex end results of that unscrupulous manipulation or adulteration of our food is called obesogens.

These are foreign chemical compounds *"that disrupt normal development and balance of lipid metabolism, which in some cases, can lead to obesity. ...they disrupt energy balance or modify the regulation of appetite and satiety..."*

(Wikipedia)

That these foods are fattening is now an accepted truth. But do we know what will be the repercussions or the long term fallouts of these bionic foods on our kids' bodies still in the growing process? Are we already or will we end up genetically modified? It only started less than 20 years ago and already we see a drastic change in the population body weight and life expectation. What will it be like in another 20 years? If we end up more genetically modified, does that make us *short-lived aliens or Frankensteinians*???

Because the food is more and more fattening and the fast food restaurants have more and more appeal with the majority of people and are more accessible to the kids, it compounds the problem ten folds.

> Toronto schools to look at obesity in students: ... (it) **will look at 12,000 students from Grade 7 to Grade 12 at 160 schools across the city. It will be for data collection only. Participation is voluntary and students will only find out their BMI if they ask, and no letters will be sent to parents**.

> (web page)

I understand that it's an alarming situation and that we must diligently look into it. I get that. But I would rather be overweight and happy than skinny with a low self-esteem... So, we must be extremely careful not to launch a destructive attack on the kid's self-esteem which would only act as an accelerant in this epidemic already encompassing a large part of the student body. (no pun intended). Also, the cyber bullies don't need any more ammunitions than they already have. Being called "fatso" or "whale" can be equivalent to a death sentence as we have seen in the chapter about bullies and cyber bullying.

On the other hand, I'm deceived to see that we might still be in the dark if we believe that low nutrient and high sugar food are on top of the list in the battle against the overweight/obesity enemy which possesses weapons of mass destruction of which we know very little. It's far more complicated and technical than we suspect. Pretty soon, in order to be able to go shopping for the family and bring back edible healthy food, one will need a degree in botany, in forensics, in chemistry, in biology and in other sciences that might not exist yet!

Our neighbours to the South, the Americans, took action in a manner that I would call segregationist when in the face of that serious societal problem they isolated the kids while the percentage of overweight/obese people is twice as high among adults than among school kids.

"In the US, BMI studies in 21 states sent home letters to parents colloquially called "fat letters", telling them their child is overweight or obese."

Marc Montgomery, *english@rcinet.ca*

And to sheepishly try to justify their manipulative conduct, they retort that, because of the letters, *many* had made some changes in their habits and diet, as if it was OK *to humiliate **all** the weight challenged kids* if it did help **many** of them!

There's probably no better place to start to educate the next generation about the risks of food than in school. But, seriously, is it only a question of education? Personally, I am in favor of offering the opportunity to students to learn as much as possible about the different foods and their nutritional value. I am also in favor of informing them on how certain foods contribute to make us fat. I am in favor of informing them of the health risks of being overweight or obese. I am even in favor of giving more importance to nutrition education in school than ever before.

But, if we don't find an intelligent and humane way of doing it without making anybody feel self-conscious or singled out, we are compounding the problem ten folds! They're probably going to eat more junk food in a compensative way, for solace!

Now, let's suppose we find a way of creating such a program. At the risk of passing for an alarmist, here's what I think. We can learn all there is to learn about food and proper nutrition but I don't think it will make a big difference. It would possibly change our choices of certain foods, but it would not change the nature of the available foods.

At the moment, in 2013, I'm not sure that the most educated on food and food tampering person can go in any grocery store and find $20.00 of ok food. Why? Because, according to some estimates, there would be *as many as 30,000 genetically modified organisms on grocery store shelves in the U.S.* Usually, Canada is not far behind. I hope sincerely to be wrong about Canada.

And according to Jill Ettinger in *Everything You Absolutely Need to Know About GMOs:*

> *"Environmental degradation and food-related health issues are on the rise, and GMOs may play a critical role in causing irreversible damage to both our species and our planet."*

> Allow me to repeat: *"GMOs may play a critical role in causing irreversible damage to both our species and our planet."*

If students had the choice between learning about the population of Titicaca, in Geography, and *about food causing irreversible damage to both our species and our planet*, what would they choose? Those are extremely alarming allegations! Did you read what I read? *...irreversible damage to both our species and our planet!!!* Is it only me or is it scary? Can it be true?

Efforts to pass a law forcing the food corporations to label the GM food items as Genetically Modified Organisms have not yet bore fruits. Not only there is no law in the United States to stop what is happening, the food giants like Monsanto, DuPont, Pepsi, Coca Cola and Nestle are trying very hard to prevent such laws from ever being passed. On top of investing a lot of money to fight these laws, they are spreading a lot of misinformation.

Many scientists and prominent health agencies

"...have determined GMOs safe for consumption, including the World Health Organization, the U.S. National Academy of Sciences and the American Medical Association."

James Andrews, Food safety news.

Am I reading that right? *The World Health Organization and the American Medical Association* have determined GMOs safe for consumption? Really? Either Jill Ettinger doesn't know what she's talking about, or, Monsanto and company are not telling the truth, the whole truth, and nothing but the truth...!!!

Tragic doesn't start to describe the nature of the threat! It's more like potentially cataclysmic! If our governments don't regulate the food corporations -short of saying the food monopoly- from using extremely dangerous methods to fatten our bottom and their bottom line, I believe we're an endangered species! Maybe not me, I'm going on 77... but my kids, your kids and their kids...

However, if we the people would take our power back from the establishment and get our heads and hearts together, for a change, and boycott one or many of the products of some of the corporations at the head of this destructive machination, like Coke and Pepsi, and not buying their soft drinks, until they accept the law allowing to label the GMO products, we would see some results. There are other soft drinks than those that might not be better for you." But, indirectly, on the long run, you would be a lot better off if that new law passed because of your actions hitting the big corporations where it hurts them badly, in the back pocket.

I believe the school kids could -and probably would- join in. They have to be exposed to the threat of GMOs and supported if they decide to take some action on their own or in collaboration with adults *if they still believe we can do something right! I'm sorry to say, but we have betrayed them terribly by having thrown them under the bus (school) when they were six and still trusting us...*

Let's keep in mind that the great majority of corn and soy produced in U.S. are genetically modified. Yet soy and corn are used in a lot of processed food as a filler because it's probably cheaper than the food it replaces. GM soy and corn are becoming the magic substance that replaces real food products. That notion is important in order to understand the implications of the following quote.

> Everybody knows about or is taking vitamin C (ascorbic acid) which ...*"is often made from corn, vitamin E is usually made from soy. Vitamins A, B2, B6, and B12 may be derived from GMOs as well as vitamin D and vitamin K may have "carriers" derived from GM corn sources..."*

> Mavis Butcher, Subject Category: Fitness and Nutrition

They will stop at nothing in order to fatten their bottom line, it seems. It's a fact that our kids are a lot less active than they were, let's say, 20 years ago. And the main reason is the advent of TV and the electronic gadgets that they carry and use constantly when they have a chance. They either, watch TV, play games on the computer, listen to their music through their earphones, text messages, or chat with a friend on their cell phone. Now, if you look around when you go shopping, you'll notice that everybody is doing the same thing, *except most of the old farts like me.Lol.*

In spite of the fact that I don't believe that any amount of Phys-Ed will solve their overweight/obesity problem completely, I'm still in favor of offering them an opportunity to take a lot of Phys Ed. But it will have to be made interesting and fun and not a chore or a punishment for their weight. Sports and gymnastics could bring some normalcy and some valuable education in their student life.

23

Physical Education

"The five S's of sports training are: stamina, speed, strength, skill, and spirit; but the greatest of these is spirit."

Ken Doherty

In September 1969, I had the chance and the pleasure to teach in a brand new school, with a very modern architecture, with Phys Ed facilities, very likely a first for the whole of the Gaspé Peninsula. As far as I was concerned, a large gymnasium and two large basketball/volleyball gyms combined were a real treat. I had never seen anything like it!!! We had moved from a bicycle to a Cadillac!

As you can imagine, I was very happy to return to teaching in such a nice new school and in a new discipline. After a few months teaching all the different activities and sports,-we were 4 Phys Ed teachers- we agreed on a strategy: each of us would take one discipline and teach it for the rest of the year. I was the only one having no degree in Phys Ed. I ended up with gymnastics. I was very happy about it. I always loved gymnastics and I had done quite a bit of it in the seminary. I was far from being an accomplished gymnast, but I understood the subject well enough to teach it, and that, in a safe manner.

One of the first problems to arise was the showers in common for boys. They had never been exposed to it, and even some parents were objecting to it. They thought it was immoral or something! Girls' showers, on one hand, were separated cubicles adjacent to a locker room where to undress. They could manage it without being naked in front of others. The boys, on the other hand, had to shower naked in front of their classmates. There were problems with certain students shyer than others. I remember that one day, Régis, one of the Phys Ed Profs had tried calming down their apprehensions in these terms:

"Guys! Don't worry! Between the longest and the shortest, there's seldom more than a foot difference..."

Eventually the novelty wore off and things settled down. I had girls-only classes, boys-only classes, and mixed classes. These mixed classes could sometimes create dangerous situations when some guys would try to impress the girls, not always in a smart way. We were using a wooden box with padded top, we called a German horse. It was about 4 feet high and 4 feet long. In front of it, there was a spring board, set at the right distance from the horse. The student would stand at about 20 feet from the spring board, run, jump on the spring board, gain some altitude, put his hands on the padded top of the apparel, flip over and land on his feet on the mats.

One day, as usual for that exercise, I was standing by the German horse, at one end of it. The next student in line was a girl. She started running, jumped on the spring board, and while she was in the air, upside down, a guy grabbed the end of the German horse and pretended to pull it from under her. Distracted by that gesture and scared she would land on the floor head first, instead of on her hands on the German horse, she aborted her manoeuver and landed on her back on top of the German horse.

My job was to protect her and help her if she needed assistance. It happened very fast and I caught her at the last second. But to catch a person of about 125 lbs, at arm's length ...is very heavy. I had slowed down her fall as much as I could, but she still hurt her back. I chatted with her so that she could describe her pain to me. I decided that there was no chance to take. I warned the principal that I had to take one of my students to the hospital, which was about 8 miles away. I helped her walk to my car and I drove her to the hospital. In a few minutes, a doctor was available and after examination, having found nothing broken or displaced, he told her what to do for the pain and we came back to school. It could have been very serious. She could have broken her back. In a week or so, she was ok.

Now, what do you do or say to the 16 year old boy who pulled such a crazy and dangerous stunt on that girl? I could have sent him to the principal like most teachers would have done. I didn't. In six years, I never sent any student to the principal.

Problems happening in my class were settled or handled in the class. This way, he saw the pain on his friend's face, he saw the disapproval on other students' faces, and he saw the deception and the sadness on my face...

This way, instead of removing him from the situation he had created, he had to endure the other students' stares and live up to the consequences... and learn from it. We all do crazy things sometimes, and the real bad ones are the ones we don't learn from. To me, that's more important than knowing that Christopher Columbus discovered America...*which is not true anyway!* That student surely realized he had done something very dangerous, and he wouldn't do it again, unless he was crazy, in which case I wouldn't let him participate in gymnastics anymore. And I would recommend to the principal that this boy sees a psychologist or a psychiatrist.

To me, that a boy does something like that doesn't mean that he is stupid. It rather means that he has a poor self-esteem, that he is desperate for attention, for girls' attention, in his case. He probably hasn't learned to relate to others and therefore even less to girls. He most likely has a problem relating to others since his relation to himself is limping at best. And what he needs is not literature or history or geography. What he needs is certainly not coercion! Instead, he needs nurturing and support from his family and very likely psychological counseling to help with his interpersonal relationships if he's going to have a chance at a normal life. Otherwise he's facing a very uncertain future. The school probably didn't create his problem in the first place, but it certainly doesn't do anything to help him overcome it!

One thing is certain: his dangerous stunt didn't help with the situation of the girls who were scared of these exercises. Girls from that area had never been exposed to that kind of activities. They were scared of hurting themselves. There was something else, I believe, they were scared of. Having been raised in a prudish manner, which was part of their socio-cultural and of their religious upbringing, they felt they were exposing themselves and being indecent while doing pirouettes in Leotards, especially in front of boys. I believe most teachers would have used coercion to force them to engage in gymnastics like everybody else. I do not believe in coercion, in school, at work or in society, especially not in child education.

There would be up to 8 of them at a given time, against the wall, in their high heels and holding their purse. *"They were having their periods,"* week after week, every week! I had no Ph.D. in gynecology, but I had been living with a woman for eight years... I was facing a dilemma. I knew that their excuse of having their periods was just that: an excuse... period! And they knew that I knew. I chose to win them over, one by one, by the degree of security in the exercises I was *inviting* them to try. They could see that I was extremely vigilant so nobody gets hurt, while executing their flips and pirouettes. I was always next to the apparel in use, ready to rescue anybody running into problems. But, I would never touch a student unless he needs my intervention. I wanted them to have the entire merit of their effort, unless they were in danger. I had to be there, mind, body and soul...and I was!

"Never help a child with a task at which he feels he can succeed."

Maria Montessori

It would not have been a problem to exercise during their periods, but it would have been dangerous to force them to do certain exercises while they were paralyzed by fear. Naturally, I wouldn't have dreamt of having them start on spring boards and apparels like the German horse. I would always start with exercises on the mats that a young child can do, like somersaults. And from there, gradually move on to the next step. It was easy to see who was agile and gifted and who was stressed or mediocre. What they were asked to do was requiring creativity. One has to visualize the exercise in one's head, before doing it on the mat or on the apparel. Creativity, like producing art or loving, cannot be ordered and forced upon someone without producing the opposite effect to the one desired.

Forced creativity is destructive; destructive of an experience that should be desired, appealing, exciting, thrilling; in a word, of a spiritual nature and soul massaging! The individual comes out of forced creativity a damaged good, instead of coming out of it improved, expanded, exponentially bettered, freer, and nearly sublime! Knowing and loving self, life and others more!

That's what school could and should do for our kids! Instead it instructs, indoctrinates, molds and bores to death! It slows down self-actualization, atrophies self-esteem, and pushes to drugs, to alcohol, to mental suicide... or *otherwise*, in some cases. Not a gay picture! Therefore I decided I would use the gentle approach. I would gradually coax them to participate, giving them the opportunity to see the fun of the girls who were participating and were obviously enjoying themselves.

The girls who were gymnastics enthusiasts were doing a good job at convincing their friends to join in. Eventually, they would show up, in Leotards, they would stand in line, eventually getting closer and closer to be first in line and then ...run to the back of the line. They were not ready. They would repeat this move until they would get enough confidence and decided to go for it. Some of them would look me in the eyes and say:*"You're sure you won't let me fall, now, OK???"*

I would reassure them and finally, they would master their fear and come out of it unhurt and so proud of themselves, shouting to their friends and to themselves: *"I did it!!! I did it!!!"* I felt like hugging them. It would have been natural, heartwarming and uplifting for us both… But we were in the dark ages…amongst a dumb down population. At this point, I must open a parenthesis on a very important mechanism of human nature: fear.

I'm not sure if I mentioned that, later in life, when I would get in a manic phase, *I was scared of nothing and of nobody.* We have been raised thinking that fear is a sign of weakness, the sign of a lack of courage, something shameful we should hide from others at all cost. Well, to me, nothing could be further from the truth. Fear is not the enemy: danger is the enemy! Fear is the little friendly voice telling you:

> *"Hi, I'm your friend, Miss Fifi (for Fear). My job is to protect you from a foe I call Old Dan (for Danger) When Old Dan is lurking, stay calm, be alert, open your eyes, open your ears, open your mind; get ready for fight or flight. React, get your adrenaline going! There might be a fire in the house or… the toasts might be burning. Find out which it is, do not run away from me; do not ignore me; I am your best friend. Work with me! My job is to prevent and protect you by pointing out to you when Old Dan is around the corner! Remember: I'm your friend, I love you! PLEASE, HELP ME HELP YOU!!!"*

Instead we are taught to run away from fear or to bottle it up and defuse it. It is not normal to be fearful of the smoke alarm detector. It's noisy, but should not be scary. It should be music to our ears when it rightly comes on at four in the morning and the house is on fire. It's telling us to gather our loved ones and exit the building, *presto*!

It is normal to fear danger. And one of the big dangers is to fear …*fear!* To deny fear, to be ashamed of fear, is irrational and dangerous! And we learn that from our upbringing at home, at church, at school, in society. My church brainwashed us into believing that fear of God is the beginning of wisdom! Fearing God is fearing the supreme source of Love! In my religion of one,-me-, Life and Love are synonymous. Without Love or Life, I am no more.

To be scared of nothing and of nobody -like I was when I was high- is dangerous for me and for others around me. *Please understand me well*:

> **"I'm a human being, the most savage and dangerous creature in the creation; the only creature threatening the survival of humanity!"**

Lions, crocs and sharks do not threaten the world; *man and his lust for power and prestige and his irresponsibility threatens the world and our very existence, yours and mine!* We should be smart, and welcome our fears, and not put them in a straight jacket. If we do, we will disappear before our time!

Eventually, all my girls participated, and the ones who were scared at the beginning, had conquered their fear, and that would change their life from that moment on. Our fears, I believe, all come from one big pool in our psyche. And when we conquer one, I believe we tame all of the others, by being better equipped to face them. I was teaching to help my students grow, discover who they were, and to love themselves and others in the process.

It's sometimes difficult to know if we are helping or hindering when we choose to teach in a certain way that differs from the majority of the teaching body. *Who was I to walk to a different drum than the rest of the teachers?*

Twilight (Crepuscule)

The day is already consumed,
The sun declining far away,
On golden sea, its day resumed,
The horizon, out of the way.
.

Like the soul of a moribund
That retires in the silence,
Its gently shades of red abound,
On golden sea slowly balances.

Pure gold water seems to swallow
The silent sinking great Monarch,
Without a sound the scene mellows;
The whole nature plunged in the dark

And like the end and the outcome,
Of this drama for mother Earth
Like a curtain, down the night comes,
Thus hiding the sight of the hearth.

Roméo Gauvreau, Feb. 15 1959,
Translation, Feb. 15 2013.   (Coincidence???)

24

And man invented the wheel...

> *"Without question, the greatest invention in the history of mankind is beer. Oh, I grant you that the wheel was also a fine invention, but the wheel does not go nearly as well with pizza."*

Dave Barry

Man invented the wheel and then he invented media...*so he could brag about the wheel!* If I draw a correlation between the wheel and the media, it's because I think that the advent of the electronic information and communications has had -*and will have*- an influence on human beings, the amplitude of which we never witnessed ...since the invention of the wheel. Most people, I believe, would be surprised to hear anything possibly negative about the advent of the electronic information and communications era.

In other words the new gadgets allow instant communication between a billion and a half people on facebook alone, and access to the internet 24/7, anywhere in the industrialized world for billions of people from the very young age of maybe 5 or 6 and younger. I will not list those sophisticated hand-held devices. You know what they are. We now see more and more people with these gadgets and it only started a few years ago. What it will be like in another 10 years is everybody's guess.

Both types of computers, the stationary and the portable ones like the lap tops and the smartphones, can have potential addictive properties. One can easily spend all his free time watching videos on You Tube, wimp.com and many other sites, playing games, alone or with other people online, communicate through facebook, Skype and many other ways about which I don't have a clue. But you all know the versatility of the computer. Now, let's talk about another gadget we have in the house that is less mysterious and less threatening...or is it?

Under its harmless appearances, the television, for me, is the most fantastic... and the most dangerous of all the gadgets around! Of all the major influences on our kids' evolution, I would, without hesitation, place media among the first few. It's still too early since the advent of the media in the modern world to be able to conclude with a degree of certainty how it's going to shape societies. The industrialized world, in the last 20 years or so, has been hit by the really infectious electronic information and communication technology. It came with the speed and the impact of a level five hurricane...and it's here to stay and get to a higher level!

Between the world of the eighties and the world of 2014, there's a chasm of monumental proportions. And that, particularly -and maybe exclusively- through *the sudden explosion of information and communications that has come upon us like a fierce but welcome tsunami.* I don't think we, as of yet, know what will be the end result of that cultural shift of the axis of society.

In 1876, when the young inventor Alexander Graham Bell gave the phone to the world, he was far from knowing how far reaching his *"distance speaking gadget"* was and the world didn't totally comprehend and foresee the consequences of this apparently curious but inoffensive gadget.

With the vocal communication doors open, there was just one small step for mankind to add the picture to it. I will not try to clarify who invented television or *"distance-sighting"*, as it's been called. It appeared on the market about 75 years ago. It was like the wheel had just been re-invented! Gradually it invaded our homes, first in black and white, then in color and then... in clusters. Most houses have now 3 or 4! Why do I make such a fuss about it? It's only television!

One day, we'll realize that TV is a nice toy, but a toy that can be very dangerous for kids... of any age, but more so for young kids. It seems like nothing, but it's far from being as harmless as we think. Let's look at some of its most serious effects on our kids. TV engulfs them in a world of false reality, or worse, of deceitful reality, without alerting their psyche. A newborn baby can't hold an iPhone and operate it, but he can -and does- watch TV from a couple of months old to age 6. I believe we should try to avoid that at any cost. Cheap technology permits parents to have especially designed child programming that can be a lot less damaging than the junk we call television. And even a *perfect programming* for children, which does not -*and never will*- exist, has to be age-appropriate, monitored and for a controlled duration.

Even world news are often pre-censured and peppered with political and military propaganda.

> **"Commercial appeals to the people through advertising, which plays on irrational fantasies and impulses, are some of the most pervasive forms of propaganda in existence today."**

> Nancy Snow's

I believe advertising to be essential for the success of commerce. But when I see young kids and even infants exposed to the advertising manipulative techniques, it makes me shudder to see the television being used as a babysitting robot. Advertizing is an unscrupulous tool that backs off for nothing or nobody in order to reach its goal which is to manipulate the psyche of those it reaches, *whatever their age*.

Another problem is the desensitization of people towards murders, wars and sufferings that humans should not have to witness. It is said that a youngster by the age of 18, will have seen an estimated 200,000 acts of violence on TV, including 40,000 murders. TV is a school system they believe in, more than they believe in their parents and teachers in lots of cases... What are we teaching our kids???

Another trick of advertizing is to raise the volume of their commercials in order to hook us better. Their techniques demonstrate a flagrant lack of moral ethics and respect of the individuals. Naturally their lobbying our governments allows them those atrocities. But here is some good news. Pretty soon, *apparently*, there will be TV sets on the market *equipped with ...an on/off button!* It could help alleviate the problem...lol

> *"Modern propaganda exploits knowledge and the psychology and communications techniques. It favors the manipulation of the feelings to the detriment of the capacities of reasoning and of judgment."* (author's translation) (www.toupie.org,)

These, in a nut shell are my thoughts about the gadget we call television, its twisted reality and the dreaded advertizing, both efficient means of conditioning and of manipulating the masses. After having condemned the corrosive influence of TV and its questionable programming, I'll add this: even if the content of the TV programs were perfect, the practice of watching TV for hours every day constitute a serious problem for most individuals, especially for kids.

It is definitively not easy to decide what and how much each kid can watch. How to organize it when we have kids of different ages and some under age, if the TV is in the family room? There's no easy solution short of having no TV in the house. That is not easy either. As much as I have been thinking about the problem for years, I haven't come up with a solution yet. The more activities the parents share with their kids should act as a deterrent to TV watching. And not having a TV in the house or not allowing the kids any watching time could make pariahs out of the kids. That alienation from their peers could have serious consequences I wouldn't be ready to expose any kid to, unless you're Amish...

> *"What teenagers want most of all are social rewards, especially the respect of their peers."*
>
> Alison Gopnik

25

"Please don't try to remember"

"Tell me and I forget. Teach me and I remember. Involve me and I learn."

Benjamin Franklin

How crazy would a teacher have to be to give such an advice to his class: *"Don't try to remember?"* Terribly crazy ...or very different in his approach of a subject as difficult as biology. Well, I must admit that I was that crazy teacher. Before starting this oddly named chapter, must I remind you that I do not think like most people you meet in your everyday life? The best explanation that I can muster is that I'm a non-conformist. I do not follow anybody ...except at a buffet...lol. But let me share that real life experience while teaching in Carleton, Québec, in April 1967.

It must have been middle of April, when the principal invited me to his office. He was in a jam and needed somebody *"presto"* to take care of the problem at hand. The biology Prof, Nurse Smith, had fallen ill and would be on sick leave for an indefinite period of time. He needed somebody to possibly teach the last two months of this subject to her grade 11 classes. So he asked full of hope:

-*"Can you take over and replace her starting ...tomorrow?"*

I thought to myself: *"Biology! Hum! Sure, why not?"* And as if he worried I would decline the offer, he added sheepishly:

-*"The subject to teach is **reproduction**. You don't have to talk about it in class; no teacher explains it to the students, because they find it embarrassing to talk about those things to 16-17 year old boys and girls in the same group. So you can just instruct them what to study and give them tests on it and it will be okay."*

He was talking to the wrong guy... I had always been interested in biology for some curious reason. I happen to be one of those lucky guys having *a whole body for himself* ...and curious about its *"modus operandi"*... My brother was a surgeon and when I was 17, one late night, he got called to go to the hospital for an operation, at about half an hour away from home. He asked me if I wanted to go with him. I accepted, and on the way there, he turned to me and asked if I wanted to watch the operation. *What kind of question was that?*

Of course, I wanted to watch. He had just operated on me for the same problem-appendicitis-a couple of weeks before. So, I stood at the head of the operating table by the anesthesiologist side. Right there in front of me, on the table, was a bare naked 17 year old girl that had just received a clean shave for the occasion... That, in itself, was an important lesson in anatomy...

In 1957, where I came from, whatever your age, sex outside of marriage was a mortal sin, an abomination. The naked woman's body, we were told, was dirty. I heard it *from my own mother's mouth.* So, it had to be true! *This one looked fine to me...* That alone, the naked affair was quite a treat for me! Then, damn! They covered her up with a green garment with the necessary opening for the operation.

In 1957, in my area, your chance of seeing a woman's breasts, in flesh or in a magazine, was about nil. First the only magazine coming to our area was the Eaton's catalog. And in those catalogs, they were selling bras. Those catalogs were our main source of toilet paper. But not before the pages with bras had been mysteriously removed by the censure. My mother like other mothers had to make sure men didn't see a bra even on paper before they get married. There was never a bra on our clothes line even if there were 6 females in our house! I can only guess that they would put a new bra on and removed it when it fell apart... and replaced it with another one, in the dark, under their blankets!

We had no electricity, no bathroom, therefore no bath, no toilet, no running water, hot or cold, no privacy:...*no problemo*!!! And not every man could see his wife breasts after they were married either. Some wives had long gowns covering them from head to toes. They would undress in the dark, put that gown on and never removed it...even for sex. There was a hole strategically located to make procreation possible... *Not to be confounded with making love!* It was a sin for a woman to enjoy sex!!! How misogynist can a religion be??? No bull! Ask the elders...they'll remember.

As I watched with great interest and curiosity, Dr Mark explained to me every details of the procedure. I was surprised to see with which detached attitude my brother was doing the cutting, the handling and the sewing of the organs he was dealing with. It reminded me of the way my dad would fix an old pair of shoes using a contraption we called an iron foot, to hold the shoe firmly in place. It felt like if he was not operating on a human being, but just on a piece of meat detached from that young girl. And he was known as a good surgeon, and he was. When you do that routine operation a couple hundred times a year, for 10-15 years, you often work on automatic pilot.

We are now back in school and, rich of my background in anatomy... I have to get ready for the next day classes of biology. Here's how it goes. I have to prepare for the first period which I will repeat in front of three other groups. So I prepared myself properly, that night at home, and the next morning, I faced the music. There was no way I would not teach them reproduction and that, for many reasons.

First, I'm not a prude. Second, I believe that biology is of utter importance for anybody. The school system pretended that it was just one of those schedule fillers. Not to distract from the subject at hand, in time, I'll get back to what I really think of our school system. My way of looking at their priority list goes like this. That biology would be less important in their curriculum than geography and history puzzles me...

However, confident in my vast knowledge of biology, (… two hours of preparation) I entered the classroom of the first group of *guinea pigs.* I could have started like the majority of teachers do and put my name in big letters on the blackboard, point to it with a chalk and say, with authority and a bossy attitude: *"Hi! Class, my name is **Mister Gauvreau**."* Instead I said:

"Hi! Guys and girls, my name is Roméo. Mister Gauvreau was my father. So, please call me Roméo. As you might already know, Nurse Smith is on a sick leave for possibly the rest of the school year. I have been asked if I would accept to replace her and I accepted with pleasure. I don't know that I can replace her; she's a nurse and I don't know a whole lot more about biology than you do. But, with adequate prep work, I believe I can do the job. Might the future reveal that I'm a lemon and an ignorant mutt, feel free to fire me…"

Everybody laughed. At that moment, I knew I had their attention. I continued establishing a connection with them:

"I do not want you to put me on a pedestal. I'm not God… I'm only his second in command."(More laughs)

I continued by telling them that we would live an experience together, an enriching one if they agreed to play along with me. I confided in them that I hated school when I was their age and that I understood their feelings. And then they heard me say:

"Class can be boring and, most of the time, is. But I have news for you. I believe I can make this interesting… and even fun. Here's what I'm talking about. The subject we want to familiarize ourselves with is biology, but more particularly reproduction. You all know I'm not talking about forgery here, I hope….lol. With your help, I'll be attempting to talk with you about the birds and the bees' subject in a more adult and realistic way than the different versions you got from the underground information network… And since many of you might be ill at ease to hear and to talk about that "taboo" subject in front of others, I will do my best to make you comfortable by being comfortable myself—which I am— when talking about that subject that concerns and should be of interest to all of us.

I will ask you to trust me with doing something no other teacher has ever asked you to do. I'm asking you to not try to memorize what you are going to hear during biology in my class. I'll make sure you remember everything you'll hear from me. Close your books, and do not take notes, unless you really want to. I promise you, you'll remember."

You should have heard and seen their reactions! They were gasping!!! How could they remember the material without taking notes and study them by heart? I was expecting their reaction and I was prepared. To one of the students that was very likely mediocre in academic subjects—I knew that because of where he was sitting, right at the back of the class, how he was sitting and the smirk on his face—and was voicing his disbelief, I countered:

-"*What did you do last night after dinner?*"

He looked both ways at his friends, kind of meaning:"

-"*What is he talking about?*"

—"*I went outside and played with my friend Johnny, and then I went home.*"

—"*What did you do after that?*"

—"*Oh! After that, I watched a movie on TV.*"

—"*What movie was it?*"

He kept looking back and forth to his two sidekicks, kind of gesturing:

"*Where the hell is he going with that?*"

He didn't know more than the rest of the class where I was going with that line of questioning, but I knew... So I stayed with him and I was doing it with a smile, without malice or making fun of him. And I repeated my question saying:

-"*Please humor me: What was the title of the movie you watched?*"

-"*It was "The sound of music"*", he finally blurted out.

—"*Who are the principal actors?*"

—"*Everybody knows that movie...*"

I came back with:

—"*Please just play along with me and you'll understand what I'm trying to do in a moment.*"

113

After listing the main actors and what was the movie about, I asked and got the whole scenario of the movie. I had to stop him; he was on a long spiel. And then came the question that floored him:

—*"Can I see your notes, please?"*

—*"What notes?"*

—*"The notes you took during the movie..."*

—*"Are you pulling my leg, Sir? Who takes notes during a movie?"*

—*"I don't, but I thought you did because you told me you wouldn't remember biology unless you tried hard to remember, took notes and studied them! Do you have two different sets of brains, one for movies and one for school subjects? Lol. Let me explain that little experiment I did with you, and, by the way, thank you for being such a good sport."*

And now addressing the whole class, I explained to them that we do not have to make a special effort to remember the things that we enjoy and are motivated to listen to. In a word the things we are interested in, the things we're curious about. It prints itself in our mind effortlessly and stays there for a long time, sometimes for our whole life. I told that young man that in 10 years, if that movie happened to appear on his TV screen, he would immediately remember having seen it, the name of the actors and the story of the movie. Why is it that school subjects we don't like, in most cases, do not stick with us and if they do, most of them fade away in a matter of days, if not hours ...if they stick at all?

By the time I finished helping them understand my theory, which I found out later, is one of William Glasser's theories, the period was over, and I had given a great lesson in biology! Not that it was in the manual. But that it is an aspect of human behavior we call motivation brought about by curiosity. And I'm pretty sure that up to this day, they remember the out of the box conversation we had together that morning. I repeated this little experience with the 2 or3 other groups I taught biology to, and then I started the program. I had created a relationship with those young adults, those good kids, those human beings I had no reason to dislike and all the reasons in the world to like and respect, particularly in putting myself on their level. Students and teachers are both students at life and the role of each often flip flops. I will, later on, talk more in depth about the giant I call: Dr William Glasser, psychiatrist and chemical engineer. He is a leader in a coercion-less school system worldwide.

That experience in biology turned out very well as far as I have been able to see during the end of the year government exams. I was one of the supervisors. I checked the answers of many students and in the reproduction, genetics and heredity part I had taught, everybody seemed to have remembered the big words we had work at getting familiar with, not by cramming, but by repetitive use of these big words and the atmosphere of fun and relaxation I had put in place.

One doesn't learn while being bored to death, stressed, coerced, or blackmailed. And if one learns, he learns to escape and to resent his reality, face to that orchestrated dumbing down compulsory schooling we impose on him ...in the name of Education!

As for my secret, I made an effort to present the complicated subject with humor, whenever possible. It was helping with their shyness and embarrassment in front of others. I really prepared my courses and myself thoroughly, and I insisted on the subjects that were of utmost importance to them. Of those, came at the top of the list, the menstrual cycle and birth control. To me, a 17 year old girl that does not know when she can or cannot get pregnant in her menstrual cycle and how to prevent it is playing Russian roulette.

> *"Sex education is legitimate in that girls cannot be taught soon enough how children don't come into the world."*

(Author's emphasis) ***Karl Kraus***

I never taught for the school board, my employer, I never taught for the principal, my boss, I never taught for other teacher's approval; I taught for my students to whom I was committed. My duty was to try and help them as much as I could to become who they really were. Another one of my mottos I was promoting is that, if you don't love your students, you are hurting them *and should resign ...**yesterday!***

> **"Sex education may be a good idea in the schools, but I don't believe the kids should be given homework."**
>
> Bill Cosby

26

Creativity, creative writing.

"It is, in fact, nothing short of a miracle that the modern methods of instruction have not yet entirely strangled the holy curiosity of inquiry; for this delicate little plant, aside from stimulation, stands mainly in need of freedom."

Albert Einstein

I will dig in my personal experience to illustrate how, as ignorant as I was in my second year of teaching, I dared follow my instinct in teaching creative writing to a grade 9 group of kids.

In 1966, I was assigned French literature in grade nine and ten "classique" (classical course). Those students were aiming towards a B.A. degree. Having the chance to do the first four years of an 8 year course, in their village, without having to pay for tuitions or go as a boarder to a seminary like in my time, was making the acquisition of a degree a lot cheaper and easier, thus a lot more accessible.

Humans are endowed with a faculty which is so deeply intertwined within their nature that, without it, they couldn't function or survive. We call that faculty: creativity. We use it in all of our voluntary actions; it's at the root of all our decisions. It shapes our thoughts, our dreams, and our moves, from dawn to dusk, day in day out. Without it, I don't believe we could function. But that faculty seems to vary to a smaller or larger degree, depending on the individuals. In general, it seems to exist at a higher degree among youngsters than among *educated* adults. I believe that our school system, with its conformising of the students, cruelly atrophy their creativity. Part of it becomes dormant. And if we believe Albert Einstein:

"It is the supreme art of the teacher to awaken joy in creative expression and knowledge."

I opened and read their program for the year, which consisted of three words:

"Écrire un roman!" ("To write a novel!!!...???)

For a moment I thought: "There goes that stupid ministry of education, again! These kids are in grade 9, they're 14-15 years old. What are they (the ministers) thinking???"

After fuming against them (the government) for a while, I calmed down and started thinking more clearly about the challenge. Was it a novel for the class, or a novel each? I mulled over that program for a couple of days. And gradually, I started realizing that it might not be as crazy as I had first thought. They were only 14-15 and they hadn't been *completely* dumb down yet by that archaic school system! "Maybe" it was still possible. But the question remained: was it a novel each or a novel for the whole class, some kind of a group project? Pondering the question, and realizing that they had more creativity left than they would in a few more years of school abuse, I decided that with my encouragement and patient coaching, it was worth giving it a try: they would try to write a novel each!

After introducing myself as Roméo, and not Mister Gauvreau, (which was a big deal at the time), I chatted with them to create a connection, to establish a beginning of a human relationship, to really get acquainted. And then,-and only then- we have the right to try and have them share an experience or create one of their own.

When I told them what the program for the year in French lit was, I thought the ceiling would fall on our heads, so much they reacted:

-"They're crazy! There's no way we can do that. The most we ever wrote is a page or two," and on and on."

I gave them time to vent their anger and their feelings of frustration. I listened to them instead of telling them to shut up and behave. I listened while they were letting off steam. I was respecting them and their frustration. Most of them thought it was impossible and stupid. For the rest of the period, I listened to them. They were showing signs that they trusted me. They wouldn't have done it if I had brought them back to order right from the beginning of the period. And I shared with them that at their age, I would have felt the same way... although I wouldn't have been allowed to express it like they did. I trusted them; they trusted me. We had a common ground where we could share together. Now we could start to look at the challenge at hand more easily and with a clearer mind.

What they needed, I thought at the time, was not an injection of genius that would transform them into accomplished writers. That was not how I was seeing it at all. It was not an ego trip on my part either, pursuing fame for having succeeded in having grade 9 students, even a few of them, write and publish a book. I could write, and I could have helped them with their writing; I never did. Not in that way, anyway. My job, I thought, was to try and free their minds of all that negative and dumbing down indoctrination they had been exposed to in the last 8 years by their predominant culture and the school...

For the last 8 years, they had been treated like they could create nothing on their own. The best and really the most important thing I could and planned to do -for and with them- was to restore their confidence in themselves. I truly believed they could do it and I had to convey that message to them. That was my reason for opening a line of communication between me and them, between them and me. It took the best part of a month before I got the majority of them convinced enough to try. I never once in that year used an ounce of coercion. I was being there with them, sharing the difficulty of their task and the *enormity of that task*. I would have felt the same way if they had asked me to write a novel at 14-15. I had enough faith in them to counteract the lack of faith they had in themselves, as a result of 8 years of tempering of their psyche by the ambient culture and the school.

So, in due time, I started explaining to them how a book is made, physically made, that is. I had helped in the library in college with rebuilding falling apart books. I had learned how we sew the different sections of fold pages to have the total book held together. And then, how to make covers with cardboard covered with nice paper and attached them to the book with glue. I suggested to them to put a drawing on the cover, in color if possible etc. Also a table of content would be nice. Once again, I had their undivided attention. Finally, I started to talk about the writing part itself.

The hardest part, I believe, when writing a novel, is to find a subject, a story line, an intrigue, characters etc. Believe me; I know how hard it is. Knowing what I now know about book writing, I should have given them the option to write their autobiography instead of a novel. Nine months ago I published my autobiography which is a non-fiction book. I did not have to invent anything. It was either recounting the events of my life, which I remember, or writing an essay about some of my beliefs and some theories of mine, that I arranged in a certain order and fashion. To me, that's a lot easier than writing a novel. So I was aware that I was asking a lot from them.

I made clear, right from the start, that I would be ready to help them with the physical putting together of the book, but that I would not help them at all with the content or the story line of their novel. It was their baby and theirs alone. After a few weeks, I shut up and let them work.

After 2 months, many of them were engulfed in an adventure with their characters or heroes. Those who hadn't succeeded to start yet, were keeping busy trying. It was quite an experience to observe and to be part of... I could sit for the whole period, sometimes not even having one request for help. I was expecting a lot from them and I knew it. But I wanted to offer them the chance to create and feel the feeling of creating.

Out of imagination, with their creative juices, *create something coming from them alone...*

"Imagination is more important than knowledge."

Albert Einstein, *On Science*

As months went by, we had a small literary club of sort. There was a large scale of levels of creation. Some, on one end of the spectrum, were spinning their wheels without getting out of the rut of the conditioning imposed by society, while others were really engulfed in their fantastic adventures. For once, not only they were allowed to day dream; they were encouraged to do so! And some loved it so much, that they would write during other teacher's classes, because it was FUN! In my books, that's called involvement, engagement, self-actualization: *happiness!*

I could feel the energy in the classroom. It was very different from most regular subjects where students are bored to death. Boredom kills people. Creating brings them to life in a place of bliss we call happiness ...and often euphoria! Creating, like loving, is the most spiritual experience we can achieve! Writing will do that for you better than any street drugs I know of! I never tried street drugs, other than a few tokes of pot, in the last 40 years, but I have taken a ton of anti depressants and "benzos" and I still take some everyday, but believe me, nothing beats the high one experiences while creating, including creative writing. And, as a bonus ...*there are no withdrawal symptoms!*

The way I was helping them was by trying to create an atmosphere propitious to creativity. My faith in them was love of them in its purest form. They were strong of their creativity being acknowledged and encouraged for once! They were strong of the empowerment that this coercion-free experiment was making possible.

A phenomenon I couldn't have seen coming, happened this way. Certain novels from the most prolific writers started to resemble TV soaps. At the beginning of the class, novels were changing hands, in order to see where the story was at, since the last class. Because, at that stage in their adventure, as I mentioned, they didn't work on it in my class only, but in other teacher's classes, and also at home, at night, it seems. In a normal class, that frenzy of exchanging and reading their friends' last creations would have been curtailed right away.

To have a normal class, one needs a normal teacher. However I was not a "normal" teacher and this was not a "normal" class. I had too many memories of what were "normal" classes during my 9 years in the Gaspé seminary... to repeat that mean behavior on my worst enemies. Definitely not on innocent kids, nice kids, human beings on the road to becoming fully themselves, if we got out of their way and stop pulling the rug from under their feet constantly!

To cut a story short, for most of them, the year went like a dream. Most of the students loved it and I totally enjoyed it. The ones, who, for some reasons, didn't succeed to write a novel,-maybe five or six of them- it was not really fun. But they never got pushed or coerced in any way. I encouraged, I never showed discontentment with any of them. Writing a novel is an art that can be learned, by trial and errors, by people who have a certain facility and possession of the language, *but most importantly, by "motivated people".*

We can no more command creativity and art execution that we can command love. Either, "A", we create a propitious creative ambience for the individual, or "B", we atrophy creativity. That's in that "A" atmosphere that the writing of these novels took place.

> *"It was only when I found myself writing things I didn't realize I knew that I said, 'I'm a writer now.' The novel had become an incentive to deeper thinking. That's really what writing is—an intense form of thought."*
>
> Don DeLillo

And allow me to reproduce a quote I heard in the late fifties and never forgot:

"Ubi amatur, non laboratur, etsi laboratur, labor etiam amatur."

Which loosely translates by:

"Where there is love, there is no labor, and if there is labor, the labor itself is loved."

(Author's translation)
St Augustine

The fact that, after 55 years, I still remember that quote that I didn't have written anywhere, proves my point. That I remembered that quote for so long, doesn't speak first of my memory, but of my love for good quotes and of literature in general. I have a good memory, except about what happened 10 mins ago... lol. But I have a passion for reading and especially writing, and I love good quotes. Nobody is talented in all the different arts. There is more than one prerequisite to performing an art.

Where do we get our aptitudes and motivation from? First, we get born with a genetic inheritance, that contains some of our parents DNA, and a whole set of archetypes from hundreds of thousands of years of human race's living experiences and learning and traumas, and evolution. They are still shaping our psyche even if we're not aware of their existence. And this is in no way a scientific explanation, but I like to think that it's close enough to the truth.

That inheritance, nature's gift, mixed with our upbringing, the nurturing part of it, makes us all unique. There has never been another human being just like you, or the rest of the individuals born on this planet or anywhere else for that matter. Because of that multiple inheritance and nurturing experiences, we are all different from each other and gifted differently. *But we are all gifted.* Those gifts, most of the time, get crushed or atrophied by the process of education, as much at home in some cases as in school in most cases. So, some

123

tastes can be encouraged, left alone, or squashed. A French quote about child rearing, goes something like this:

"We cannot succeed at child rearing; we can only do as little harm as we possibly can."

Anonymous.

Same as with the Hippocratic Oath: *"Do no harm!"* Another example of taste killing in children went like this. When I was young, I would often hear that country and western music was laughable and that guitar was a ridiculous musical instrument, not worthy of the name of musical instrument. *It was not a piano!* It didn't turn me off loving guitar music, but it certainly didn't encourage me to learn how to play the guitar!

Our people had been conditioned and dumbed down by their culture that was predominantly of peasant and religious background. If, as parents, we had the wisdom of keeping our mouth shut, 90% of the time, in our children's presence, we would render them a great service. If we taught them by example instead of by instructions and preaching, our kids would have a far better chance of being less negatively and hurtfully programmed than we have been...

By the end of May, I remember depositing 22 nice handmade little books on the principal's desk: *a pile ye high!* That was the number of completed novels of my class of young writers. There was nearly a month of school left. I couldn't say the exact number of those who completed the assignment, but everybody wrote something. Maybe 4 or 5 of them never succeeded to write something we could call a novel. But, we cannot all be like Ernest Hemingway... Maybe he sucked at piano playing or at sculpting...lol.

As far as the kids who didn't succeed at writing their novel, in my books, they didn't fail. They spent a school year at two periods a week, finding out that novel writing was not their forte. When you are working towards a B.A. degree, your writing skills are important. There is a whole lot more about writing than creative writing. As long as you possess the skill of writing in good English and reading at a normal to above average skill level, you should be able to succeed in most liberal professions. Doctors and agronomists and even teachers, will never be asked to write a novel. If you teach English lit., you should possess an above average mastering of the language.

I was teaching lit to these kids, even teaching them how to write a novel! I had never, at the time, written a 10 page piece, except a booklet of poems of about 50 pages or so in 1960 when I was 22 and it had been composed over a period of 5 years. And even to this date, I never wrote a novel. Could I write a novel? I have a good enough imagination, I think, I love writing, but, so far, I am not really interested in writing fiction. The motivation is not there. And motivation is paramount to executing any art. To bring an end to that beautiful life enriching experience, both for my students and for myself, there is a punch line to the story.

Sometimes, in the beginning of June, a publishing company came to visit the school, for some kind of book promotion. They heard about my precocious writers; they asked to see some of their novels, and offered to publish three of them. The kids found out that a book publisher—in those days- could change the title, overhaul the chapter's order etc. My writers said: *"No way!"* Then they even offered publication without corrections... *Apparently* they all refused! I heard about it from the teacher who was involved in the publishing house visit, *days after the whole affair was over...*

That adventure of helping a group of young human beings *-still salvageable...* from the destructiveness of the school system-experiment the magic and the euphoria of creativity *channeled through and boosted by* their imagination remains the most endearing memory of my teaching years.

Having left Carleton 6 years later, in order to relocate to Vancouver British Colombia, I didn't have the opportunity to follow their personal journey. Claude L. who had written a decent novel, informed me that, years later, he had written his family's genealogy and had it published. He had kept excellent memories of his novel writing while he was 14. I'm still in contact with Claude via email and by sending him my books.

In 1984, while visiting the area, I went to a funeral home in Nouvelle, my own village, following the death of my sister in law's brother. Stuart, the deceased, was Lizzie's brother. I knew him well and I had taught to his daughter and his two sons.

Somebody approached me, smiling: "Do you remember me?" She was a beautiful young woman about thirty years old who seemed familiar to me, but I couldn't put a name on her face. She was one of my students. That much I knew. She told me her name and added: *"I was in your class in grade 9 classical and you helped us write a novel."*

We hugged tenderly for a moment and we started revisiting the good moments of that experience we had shared. She had been married and divorced, with two kids, if I remember well. She was a social service career woman. After a few minutes of chitchatting, she announced like that:

"I'm going back to university this coming fall."

When I asked her in what subject, she answered:
-*"In creative writing."*
And without missing a beat, she added:

"Writing that novel in grade nine with you is the thing I did in my life that made me feel the happiest ever."

Moments like that in a teacher's life are not very frequent and it touched me deeply. I had contributed to change the life of an individual, of that young girl, now a grown up woman, who was very well spoken and who knew what she wanted in life. It was life making full circle around me! That teaching experience happened 48 years ago, but it will never fade away from my best memories!

27

Homeschooling, Unschooling.

"The home is the first and most effective place to learn the lessons of life...Nothing can take the place of home in rearing and teaching children, and no other success can compensate for failure in the home."

David O. McKay

Motivated by the numerous problems or perceived problems of our public school system, some parents choose not to enroll their kids in school. Instead, they choose to keep them at home and take the onus of their education on themselves. It's called homeschooling.

The children follow the school curriculum and are tested by the school system in order to get their passing grades. It's not for every parent and for a good reason. It's very time consuming and one needs to be very resourceful. In most cases, it's the mother who takes it on her shoulders and chooses to put her career on hold.

Homeschooling is not accepted in every country. Among the countries where homeschooling is legal and who have the most prevalent homeschooling, we find Australia, Canada, New Zealand, the United Kingdom, and the United States. It's been outlawed in Sweden and Germany. It's easy to understand that its practice would be controversial, and that, for many reasons.

If we accept the argument from John Taylor Gatto saying that the compulsory schooling has a hidden agenda which is to prepare a generation of people easy to manage as citizen, factory employees, soldiers etc., we have good reasons to question the validity of the school system. As mentioned earlier, the school system is:

> *"...a deliberate scheme to outfit the pupil, not with the capacity to weigh ideas, but with a simple appetite for gulping ideas ready-made. The aim is to make 'good' citizens, which is to say, docile and uninquisitive citizens."*

> H.L. Mencken

One of the strong objections to homeschooling is the presumed lack of socialization of the kids. As it turns out, that fear seems completely unfounded. Very often, homeschoolers have activities with other homeschoolers, go on frequent field trips and have more time and opportunity to spend with friends and family.

For those who are not sure about the difference between homeschooling and unschooling, Sarah Boesveld, in the National Post, tells us that unschooling is *"...a concept that offers no curriculum to conquer, no grade levels to pass, no rules to follow. While homeschool brings the classroom to the homefront, unschooling ditches the formal studies altogether."*

And without missing a beat she adds: *"You remove the walls of the classroom, and the world becomes your learning space".*

At the risk of repeating myself, I firmly believe and suggest to the school system authorities a better way than filling the kids' jugs with questionable knowledge. We must try to expose the kids to environments and situations in which they will, by themselves, experience feelings and emotions, discover self and its quasi limitless potential. Through the drive to learn, which is inherent to their nature, they will be given the opportunity to learn the natural way. And by natural way, I mean the way their being has been designed and not the way the establishment has, in a capitalistic way, chosen to interfere with human nature for its own selfish interests.

>*"The illiterate of the future will not be the person who cannot read. It will be the person who does not know how to learn."*

AlvinToffler

I can't agree more with him. If we stop tampering with the natural curiosity and appetite for learning that is fundamental to all kids, given the modern electronic tools, now at the finger tips of the industrial country kids, they should learn what they need to know to face what's coming ahead. And what's coming ahead, we don't know more than they do, and probably less. But cybernetics and informatics will be the vehicle for it. When one knows how to learn, one will probably know how to adapt to a constantly changing future. And a constantly changing future seems to be what's in store for them. What life will be like on earth in *10 years*, we can only do projections; nobody knows.

In *The Path Less Taken*, Jennifer Mc Grail tells us that children who are unschooled are not pressured into learning and ridiculed if they don't do well:

>*"They're learning because that's what children do. That's what all humans do, unless they, like so many of us, had their natural love of learning squashed out when they were young by being told how and when and what to learn."*

28

The Socio-cultural Inertia.

"The chains of habit are too weak to be felt until they are too strong to be broken."

Samuel Johnson *(1709 - 1784)*

It's been said again and again: *"We're social animals."* We tend to live in groups which, looked at as a whole, we call societies. What does inertia-which is a property of masses in motion or at rest-has to do with societies and their culture? In order to refresh our memory about that notion of inertia, here is a definition from Wikipedia:

> *"Inertia is the resistance of any physical object to a change in its state of motion or rest, or the tendency of an object to resist any change in its motion (including a change in direction)."*

You can see the analogy between an object resisting a change in its direction and a society resisting a change in its beaten path or incrusted culture. As members of that society, we are creatures of habits. Not only do we find it difficult to change some of our habits when we want to, but *most of the time, we do not want to*. If we accept that as the truth, why wouldn't we want to, especially when we agree that it would be beneficial to us?

There's probably more than one cause for that surprising behavior. But, in definitive, it's the fear of the unknown versus the comfort of the *status quo* providing us with a kind of security blanket. It's easier to follow the beaten path than the unfamiliar path of the non-conformist.

We tend to feel more secure following *"the gang,"* even when the gang's behavior is destructive like in the case of oppression, racism, or war... *"There's strength in numbers"* is a slogan that is imprinted in our psyche, probably from eons ago. It was probably truer then, than it is now. I tend to believe that it's not the number anymore that provides us *real* strength compared to *perceived* strength.

I rather believe that it's a deprogramming and a certain knowledge that can procure us security. Knowledge of self first and knowledge of the other by extension; they're interconnected. We can't have one without the other. And for me, that's the highest form of knowledge accessible to man. We have been raised hearing a phrase that our religion was hammering us with:

"What good is it for man to conquer the universe if he ends up losing his soul?"

I can agree that it isn't worth losing our soul over material gain. However, I don't think I have the same definition of *"soul"* as they have... *Mine comes with a tether ...that guarantees you'll never lose it... Lol.* So I parody that quote and adapt it to my beliefs:

"What good is it for man to get to know everything if he doesn't know self and his fellow man?"

The prevalent cultural current was to motivate people toward the acquisition of knowledge, specially, math, science and language. With time, it ended up becoming a kind of high society passport. We saw waves of pedantry or a kind of affectation in one's way of speaking and writing. There was -and still is to a certain extent- a certain snobbery about knowledge in general. Even to this date, one is still looked at as less than competent if he doesn't have a grade 12 *education*, which, for me, means nothing.

A grade 12 education opens doors for some A and B students in the pursuit of a higher scholar education, but by no means guarantees success or happiness. And it says nothing about the individual's potential. Look at Jesus, as far as we know, he didn't even know his multiplication tables or algebra... I'm surprised our culture didn't call him a retarded!!! In our modern society, *he wouldn't qualify for the job of garbage collector...*

That cultural inertia is common to every people on earth. In lots of ways, it's a combination of indoctrination and insecurity. We find a trail used by the majority, and we accept to follow it, in spite of the fact that, very often, it doesn't really suit us. But, for the tranquility of mind and the false security it provides us with, we are ready to renounce to ever daring to follow our own star and ever becoming who we really are. In doing so, we betray ourselves. In a word, we largely prostitute ourselves for a false security because of the fear of the unknown. It was also because -and mainly because- of the *de-formation* that has been forced on us by our school's coercive straight jacket, where we were taught to obey, to conform and to sacrifice our need of individualization for the benefit of the ***All Mighty Establishment!***

That's why it's so hard to engage people in something new like a school system in which we don't use our authority as a Damocles sword over our kids' heads for 12 years of their burgeoning life. That also explains why it took over 7 years to implant a *"Quality School"* in Moncton New Brunswick, Canada. That same socio-cultural inertia explains why man, after hundreds of thousands of years of evolution-or stagnation-has not yet learn to co-exist harmoniously with his brothers of the earth and still wars against them.

So what am I saying? Would it be losing our time to try to change the culture in our society? As much as it will demand a lot of effort on our part and that it will take some time, it can be done, a step at a time, if we apply love and cooperation at the right place.

"Habit is habit, and not to be flung out the window by man, but coaxed downstairs, a step at a time."

Mark Twain *(1835 - 1910)*

The worst place where we could try to bring about some changes-*any changes*- would be to expect the government to change. It won't happen until, we, as citizen, change! The second worst place would be the church. Most are supposedly interested in humanities but in a cultish kind of way. Correct me if I'm wrong, but they all swear that they have the Truth...and are the only ones to have it.

The third worst is the school. The fact that our schools need so much improvement is not the principals, the teachers or the parents' fault. They are victims of a political and capitalist way of looking at children first as a future asset for the industry, and as an easy herd to manage as voters and soldiers! Finally, the most important place is the family.

Why the family? Let's dream for a moment and pretend that the government decides to fix the problem of compulsory schooling. First they pass a new law making school non compulsory. Surely, some kids would stop to go. I don't know how serious would the exodus from school be. I presume that, at the beginning, it might be quite significant. Eventually, though, things would get back to *abnormal.(*I nearly said normal...*)*

The school would still be a concentration camp, but without *the mental barb wires.* Now, not willing to lose all the students and look bad, the teachers might improve their attitude with the students. They wouldn't afford to be mean and bully them anymore, because the students could walk out in the middle of the teacher's sentence and give him the major finger salute. The teachers who were coercion adepts, would probably lose lots of students in their classes unless they change their approach. But most teachers don't know of another approach. They just know the coercive approach and they would have just lost their whip!

Well, there's a good ending to that story. In 1993, William Glasser found the first *"Quality School"* in the world. It's still operating to this day in Huntingdon, Wyoming, USA and in most countries around the world. What does he call a *"Quality School"*?

29

"Quality Schools"

"My children are what matters to me. And at the end of the day, if they go to sleep happy, confident, and knowing with every fiber of their being that they are loved, valued, and respected, then I've done my job."

Jennifer McGrail, The path less taken

John Taylor Gatto was a school teacher who won the *"Teacher of the year"* award four times while teaching in the state of New York. After thirty years of teaching he quit and started touring the States, lecturing on the American school system.

I share his views of a prison-like school, based on a corrosive mental conditioning, having as a result an assembly line where the end product is a diminished and subjugated individual. This would deliver an individual fitting the political and industrial establishment agenda. It was hitting me like a breeze of fresh air. *Wow!!!* He published a book titled:*"Dumbing us down."* It had, as a subtitle: *"The hidden Agenda of compulsory schooling".*

According to Dr. William Glasser, and such as applied in his *"Quality Schools"*, after grade 3 and the memorization of the multiplication tables, **memorization is no more required nor rewarded!** And the success of his *"Quality Schools"* has been largely proven across the world.

I believe we have the moral duty to get informed more deeply on a subject that has the potential for changing our children's lives, our life and the future evolution of society as a whole. In the last two centuries, by the bias of indoctrination, we have succeeded in dumbing down nearly everybody from most societies around the world.

The governments with propaganda and misinformation have controlled every country's populations. The coercive compulsory schooling has played a major role in dumbing down populations. Some religions have used indoctrination with half truths and pure phallocratic teachings and brainwashing to control the masses. In doing so, they have encouraged the subjugation and the exploitation of women all over the world and they're still doing it in most parts of the world. Happily enough, with the feminist liberation movement, women have *nearly* regained their status of equality with men in some of the industrial countries. There's still some work to be done, but we, as a society, have made a big step in the right direction.

Please allow me to repeat the quote from the beginning of this chapter:

> *"My children are what matters to me. And at the end of the day, if they go to sleep happy, confident, and knowing with every fiber of their being that they are loved, valued, and respected, then I've done my job."*
>
> *Jennifer McGrail, The path less taken*

What if for every year spent in school, starting in kindergarten, each and every kid would have been the object of respect on the part of every teacher, no matter what, for every minute of every day, wouldn't the respect of self and of others have permeated the atmosphere of that classroom and influenced our kids and their parents in a positive way? And if that atmosphere of mutual respect would have continued to exist from grade 1 to grade 12, can you see a possibility that maybe, *just maybe*, we might have less societal problems later on? Like: *less alcohol and drug problems, less violence, less murders, less suicides,* **less wars, maybe?**

If such conditions existed also at home, it would really reinforce that atmosphere of respect of self and of others that the kids need to learn in order to achieve self-actualization and, consequently, happiness.

Naturally, we don't have statistics to support or hinder the veracity of my hypothesis. Now the content of the curriculum is very important. Well, if you allow me, I'll rephrase that: the content of the curriculum *should be very important for the kids; but* never as important *as the spirit in which it is presented to the kids.*

If the minister of education of British Columbia or from any other province, for that matter, was to read my book, he would be fast to undermine my theories and would try to reassure you and me that Canada has one of the best education systems in the world, and blah, blah, blah!

The minister of education could be right. But it might only mean that the education systems of the world have nothing to brag about! There again, I recognize the fact that they all make possible the learning of the three Rs in the first three years or so. Where I have a problem, is not first what they do or do not deliver in the matter of knowledge. It's not the *what*; it's the *how*! If they could deliver a doctorate after grade 12th, I would still see our education system as extremely deficient and as a dumbing down factory.

I totally disagree with that practice of treating kids differently at school than at home. There's no reason not to try and treat the kids in a way that makes them feel loved valued and respected at all times. And if our schools cannot provide those prerequisites to education, they should close their doors and give room for the implantation of *"Quality Schools"* or for something even better!

What I would like to see happen, is the parents getting informed on alternative school systems like the Montessori schools, private schools or even homeschooling and un-schooling, whenever possible. Only a minority of parents believe they have those options. I will get back to homeschooling and un-schooling in a subsequent chapter. One option that everybody has is to demand for the generalized implantation of the William Glasser's *"Quality Schools"*. At the moment, it's by far the best option available to everybody in a distant future. Not that it is a perfect school system; there's no such thing as a perfect school system. *Perfect* and *school system* in the same sentence is an oxymoron!

We need more people to train in the Glasser's RT and CT basic and advance training to become certified counselors. One of them, with the collaboration of a school principal, can start the process of implanting a *"Quality School"* in one of the actual schools. This intense, mostly weekends, training cannot be completed in a period of less than 18 months. Taken full time, it would take around four weeks. But learning to think and to deal differently with others doesn't happen overnight! Hence the 18 months period minimum required.

So, before implanting the *"Quality School"* system, we must implant this new way of thinking and of behaving with others, especially with students. It needs some preparation on the part of the school principals, the teachers, the students and even the parents. First everybody from the janitors to the bus drivers must familiarize themselves with the Edward Deming lead management theory and with the William Glasser RT and CT principles. The Edward Deming *lead management* philosophy, in a nutshell, recommends the abolition of the use of coercion in any kind of relationship with others, at work, at home and in school. The teacher is no longer a boss to fear, but a guide and an assistant to the student.

To abandon coercion requires changing certain ways of thinking and doing which are deeply incrusted in us. The most important and the most difficult one of these ways of thinking, is the belief that use of constraint with kids is necessary to keep the control of the class and is even good for them; *"It teaches them obedience to authority and discipline."* That they learn to obey, they have no choice. As for learning discipline, that's wishful thinking... The bossing has to stop completely, on the part of everybody at home and at school. And that is a point of contention with the teachers, mainly. They fear to lose control over their classes.

All they need to do is to research what has been -and continues to be done- in many countries around the world, including Canada. That should convince and reassure them that in that *"Quality School"* system, discipline is less of a problem than in the conventional school system. As a matter of fact, class discipline is not an issue for the *"Quality School"* teacher. Teaching becomes a lot easier both for the teachers and for the kids.

And what I'm talking about here is not wishful thinking, it's not theories; those are verifiable facts. This is reality for some parents, teachers and kids in many countries around the world in 2014, right now! An important point to underline is the fact that it doesn't cost more to the tax payers and therefore the government doesn't object to it.

I'm no anthropologist, but if you asked me what the number one problem in society is, I would say... that I don't know for sure but that I really believe that it has something to do with coercion first and with indoctrination second ...or vice versa. We find those two culprits in every country around the world and we know what kind of societies it promotes.

A good way to see the possibility that it might work, is to remember how William Glasser's principles, applied in his *"Quality Schools"*, change these schools completely. Or better still, go and visit one of his schools if there's one in your area and you will realize that all is not lost.

The human spirit is very resilient and ready to bounce back, given an opportunity. To find out if there's such a school in your area, look for *The William Glasser Institute* on the web and ask about *"Quality Schools"* locations and you should find out. The one in your area might not be certified yet. It takes many years of effort in order to turn a regular school into a *"Quality School"*. In Canada, the only accredited one that I know of is in Moncton, New Brunswick, and it took many years before it was certified. In these *"Quality Schools"*, the drop-out rate and the bullying are nearly non-existent. But students are being respected at all times, no matter what.

William Glasser is a very well known and respected psychiatrist all over the world. He is well known for his successful methods in psychiatry and his elaborated investment in child education which has resulted in his founding and implementing of the *"Quality School"*. His implanting of *"Quality Schools"* in United States, Canada and in a lot of countries all over the world is very well known and documented in the publication of a few books on the subject. One of his books I read is called: *"The "Quality Schools", Managing students without coercion."*

The difference between a regular school and a *"Quality School"* is not much in the container, the school building, but in the content or the class atmosphere. Also the attitude of the teacher is very different from the one found in our antiquated schools. Students are not bossed around for one and there is no coercion used against them. There is no memorization required or rewarded after grade 3 and the study of the multiplication tables. There is no grade lower than a "B".

A "B" means competent work. Anything that is not viewed as competent yet receives an *"unfinished work"* grade. All tests are done with open books. You only get marks if you understand the material taught. Nobody gets sent to the principal or thrown out of school. Only pertinent subjects are taught in class. Any subject that wasn't of any use for you in life, got removed from the curriculum. And there is no imposed home work. You can choose to bring some, if you want to, to catch up on a subject of your choice.

The school will not call your parents if you act up in class. Every problem that happens in the school is settled in the class by a comity composed of the class members in collaboration with the teacher. If you start disturbing consistently, you will have the opportunity to meet with a counselor which will talk with you -*and not to you*- as a friend. He will chat with you and try and help you until you are ready to rejoin the group. There are usually reasons why a student starts acting up in class and often it comes from a problem at home for which he needs help and support. Not blackmailing, ridiculing, belittling and even bullying on the part of the teacher. *That never helped and never will!*

30

The make-up of a Teacher

> *"If a country is to be corruption free and become a nation of beautiful minds, I strongly feel there are three key societal members who can make a difference. They are the father, the mother and the teacher."*

Abdul Kalam

I have been referring to the function of a teacher as a *co-parent*. To be the trusting parents of a kid to the point of accepting to leave him in the care of a school where *strangers* will dictate the kid's every move and indoctrinate him for 6 hours a day for 12 years, is a great honor ...for the teachers. But *it's a sign of subjugation and irresponsibility on the part of those same parents.*

> *"Education begins at home and I applaud the parents who recognize that they - not someone else - must take responsibility to assure that their children are well educated."*

Ernest Istook

Like any other government organization, the school system, the schoolboard and the school should not be trusted by those who have the responsibility of the kid's welfare: the parents.

Not the government, not the schoolboard, not the teachers! The government is trying to operate the school system for a minimum number of dollars with as little complaints from the voters as possible.

We must re-examine the school system which, in great part, functions like any other government ministry. They (the ministers) don't care more about education than they care about you and me; **they care about being re-elected.** They want to be re-elected because *they thirst for power.* They thirst for power because *they have a huge ego. Some of them are probably sociopaths.*

> **"Yes, politicians are more likely than people in the general population to be sociopaths. I think you would find no expert in the field of sociopathy/psychopathy/ antisocial personality disorder who would dispute this..."**
>
> Dr Stout, Huffington Post

Let's get back to our teacher. If we believe that the three key societal members who can make a difference are the father, the mother and the teacher, let us remove anybody else from the equation. Let's assume that the father and the mother are good parents. I'll come back later to give my definition of a good parent. So we have two thirds of the equation in place: the father and the mother. Now we need a good teacher to complete the equation. What is a good teacher?

I could go into a long diatribe and use a lot of *"pathos!"* But I'll spare you *the bull* ! There is only one kind of teacher. Because what we call a bad teacher is *anything but* a teacher. He doesn't deserve the name of teacher. Therefore a good teacher, or, a teacher for short, (2) is a person with personal integrity bringing to the table certain attitudes and attributes. *He must love children unconditionally and* **he must not use coercion in the class or anywhere else in presence of the students**.

He must also, refuse to indoctrinate. He must avoid at all cost the brainwashing or the conditioning of the children's psyche i.e. *dumbing them down*. He must also be aware that he has a lot more to learn from observing the child than the child has from observing him. *He is not the most important person in the room; **the child is!***

> **"We discovered that education is not something which the teacher does, but that it is a natural process which develops spontaneously in the human being".**
>
> Maria Montessori

If you find such a teacher in your child's life, treat him with great respect. Because both you (the parents) and him can form *the most important team on earth towards the actualization of a genuine human being: your child.*

As for the definition of a good parent, they must have the qualities of the teacher plus love of each other to create an atmosphere of love, peace and security for the child. This love between the father and the mother is of utmost importance for the child self-esteem and self-love. If your child has self-esteem and self-love, congratulate each other with a high five! *You just succeeded brilliantly at the most difficult job in the world!*

> **"Every word, facial expression, gesture, or action on the part of a parent** (or teacher) **gives the child some message about self-worth. It is sad that so many parents** (and teachers) **don't realize what messages they are sending."** (Parenthesis is author's addition)
>
> Virginia Satir)

Together with that teacher, you are the rarest and the most sought after artists that the world will ever produce!

31

The science of human relationships

> *"If civilization is to survive, we must cultivate the science of human relationships - the ability of all peoples, of all kinds, to live together, in the same world at peace."*

Franklin D. Roosevelt

In order to cultivate the science of human relationships we can choose any or all of our sacred institutions: family, school, religion, government. As you guessed it, we can eliminate the government...unless you want to cultivate *the science of deception!*

If you choose religion, there is a great chance that you will only accomplish a dumbing down of people through indoctrination. Most religions have good intentions when they say: *"Love thy neighbor as thyself!"* I agree 100% with that good advice, but that's all I agree with. Dumbing down people is an obstacle to civilization. By teaching people to blindly obey orders and respect authorities,-*any authorities*- we prepare them for servility and domestication. The establishment is craving those attributes among the population. It makes possible their *unscrupulous manipulation of the bleating masses...*

So the government won't do it, the religions won't do it. We are left with the school and the family. As we have seen, the school with its coercive methods, as a whole, is far from cultivating the science of human relationships. It could do it if it accepted to renounce to coercion and to put in place the model implemented by Dr. William Glasser and Dr. W. Edward Deming in the *"Quality Schools"*. These are known all over the world, but it's a long process that, up till now, has been left to the initiative of *an elite* of progressive school principals and teachers.

Once a *"Quality School"* has been certified, usually after 5 to 8 years of hard work to deprogram the principals, the teachers, the students and everybody involved with these students, we have the base for their re-education. And I mean deprogramming everybody involved with the kids. Then and only then, it can finally apply the science of coercion-free human relationships. But to achieve that level of civilization, it needs a partner: the first institution.

The first institution is the family. We have come full circle. The family, at the moment is the only one of our institutions that can deliver a certain quality of relationships in spite of the other institutions. If the family chooses a coercion-free approach based on unconditional love to raise their kids, we are witnessing a cell of society with a particular twist: it's a *civilized* cell of society. Anything else is but a travesty of civilization.

Having established my belief that coercion is the downfall of education *and by extension of civilization,* we know how to remedy it. Let us give back to family the place it deserves in society: *the first place.* Here's how it should work.

First, society gives the best seats in the house to the family. The family gives the best seats in the house to their children. The family decides if their kids will attend public school. If he goes to public school, the school gives the best seat in the house to the children. If the family decides to raise their kids in a religion, it chooses meticulously for one that respects kids, do not indoctrinate them and uses no coercion i.e. *threats of hell or other fallacies...*

*I talked with God the other day, and He swore to me, "cross your heart and hope to die," that He never threatened anybody with hell... Anyway, He said unions got in hell and organized the boiler engineers with the results that they can't afford to keep the furnaces going any more. **"The hell with it"**, said He, and closed* *the damn place down... There! That should take care of Hell once and for all!*

Eons ago, people from advanced countries all knew for a fact that the earth was flat. So when one day, *an idiot*, not respecting the establishment's commonly accepted knowledge, muttered that the earth was round and turned around the sun, everybody knew he was an anarchist,...a revolutionary and a dangerous non-conformist! Who would dare advance a theory of heliocentrism when the catholic church, (the small "c" is intended) **because of its infallibility,** *knew without a shred of a doubt that the earth is flat!!! Who was he to dare declare that:*

"The earth is round and turns around the sun!"

He might as well have said that the pope was an idiot...He got the same reaction from him anyway! Not only the whole world thought he was crazy, they saw him as a threat to **the established order.** *The catholic church decreed that he would therefore be* **anathematized!** Galileo was *forced* to recant and do penance...

It's not the number of idiots that makes the strength of an argument!

32

Utopia

*"There is something very utopian about what I do.
But utopia is nothing more than a truth that the world
is not yet ready to hear."*

Yann Arthus-Bertrand

My goal in writing this book is not to try to instruct you or to indoctrinate you. It's rather to present you with a menu of theories, reflections and certain facts concerning civilization and its difficulties in advancing to the next level. That next level, for me, would be to take heed of and to put into practice the 2600 year old Golden rule:

"Do unto others as you would have them do unto you".

It's a rule that everybody understands, but somehow, we have not yet succeeded to apply it at all levels of the world's societies. Family is the institution where we apply it the most; although more in some than in others. The school is an institution where the golden rule is sacrificed in great part due to its coercive approach and its lame pedagogy. The government is the institution where it's the least applied, due to corruption and abuse of power, and the omnipresent coercion towards other countries and towards its own citizen. Is it to say that we're doomed and that there's nothing to be done?

I have a cautious optimism that reminds me that mankind, in spite of its downfalls, have shown encouraging signs that it wants to advance further in civilization. We have witnessed a certain degree of women liberation in most industrial countries, the abolition of capital punishment in Canada and in 18 American states. Of the 195 independent states that are UN members, 155 have abolished the death penalty.

Also there is a worldwide effort by various movements to save endangered species, to save the rain forests, to preserve the oceans and all water bodies from industrial and civilian pollution. Lots of people are concerned about global warming and try to push the government to put in place new measures to reduce the carbon footprint. Last but not least, we're witnessing the recycling effort around the world. I hope we succeed in slowing down the global warming of the planet, in favor of *speeding up the Global Warming of the Hearts.*

It's a fact that *"Quality Schools"* don't use coercion. It's a fact that in order to implement that coercion free system everybody dealing with these kids must also avoid coercion, from the parents to the janitors and the school bus drivers. That's the only way that it can work.

Would it be possible to extend that philosophy to an entire city?

I've mentioned *Choice Theory* as one of the important books of Dr Glasser. In 1997, he went to Corning, Colorado, and undertook the Orwellian task of teaching *Reality Therapy* and *Choice Theory* to a large part of the city's teachers and the *Choice Theory* to a large part of the citizens. He sold a thousand of his *Choice Theory* books in a city of 12,000! To me, it's a sign of great interest on the part of these citizens.

> **"Corning chose, and in a social experiment that might be utopian or Orwellian, depending on your point of view, Dr. Glasser's theories have seeped**

into many corners of this city of 12,000, tucked into a corner of the Finger Lakes region."

The New York Times
by Lisa w. Foderaro,July 12, 2002

This article by Lisa Foderaro, which I recommend to you, is giving me hope that society, given the proper education,- **not indoctrination**- can improve itself and could one day give up its barbarian customs. Among these customs, in order of cruelty, I list the wars against other countries, the civil wars (Syria, Egypt), any form of dictatorships, slavery, murders, racism, women subjugation, female genital mutilations, jails, sweat shops, compulsory coercive schooling and the list goes on. Among these, some progress has been achieved in some countries. Slavery has been mostly eradicated, while women subjugation is slowly diminishing. Women equality has made a big leap in the right direction, especially in America and a large part of Europe." But in a large part of the Middle East women subjugation is still extreme.

To remind us how difficult it is to challenge the socio-cultural inertia, lets' look at the female genital mutilation situation in the world. In the United States, one of the most industrially advanced country, F.G.M. (female genital mutilation) is illegal in 16 states. There are therefore 34 states where there is no law against it!

In Egypt, in a 2008 survey, over 90% of women between the ages of 15 to 49 years old had suffered a F.G.M. For girls between 15 and 17 years old, the percentage was **only** 74%. That percentage is expected to drop to 45 % over the next 10 years.

When I wrote **only** 74%, I wanted to underline the society's indulgence toward such a barbarian custom. To me, 74% is not **only;** it's an astronomical amount of something that should never have existed if not for the cruelty of men dumbed down by a religious and cultural indoctrination of their own doing.

On the other hand, if the F.G.M. in Egypt passed from over 90% to 74% for age group 15 to 17, there is reason for hope that the culture is accepting a marked improvement in a short period. We should not remain indifferent in the face of the plight of billions of women in the world who are treated like animals.

A society who disrespects or abuses part of its people do not deserve the title of civilized. Nearly all our modern societies disrespect their children by the bias of coercive indoctrination in school and its women, in large parts of the world, through physical and mental abuse, subjugation, F.G.M., arranged and forced marriages, honor killing, etc.

> *"[T]he legal subordination of one sex to another – is wrong in itself, and now one of the chief hindrances to human improvement; and that it ought to be replaced by a system of perfect equality, admitting no power and privilege on the one side, nor disability on the other."*

> Harriet Taylor Mill

Before ending this chapter I would like to add a word on the future of this civilization. I don't want to sound like a scaremonger, but I would like to leave you with a few thoughts about the grim prospect that humanity is facing.

> *"Now, for the first time, a global collapse appears likely. Overpopulation, overconsumption by the rich and poor choices of technologies are major drivers; dramatic cultural change provides the main hope of averting calamity."*

> *Paul R. Ehrlich*†⇓ and Anne H. Ehrlich

Among the dramatic cultural changes that we should consider seriously are curbing the warming up of the planet and the overpopulation. If the masses would be made aware of the imminent risks of overpopulation and encouraged to limit their families to no more than two children, we would see a stabilization of the population and even a decrease, possibly.

That alone would stop or at least postpone the collapse of civilization. The second threat of an imminent collapse has to do with our carbon footprint.

> *"The central challenge, of course, is to phase out more than half of the global use of fossil fuels by 2050 in order to forestall the worst impacts of climate disruption, a challenge the latest International Energy Agency edition of World Energy Outlook makes look more severe."*

> Paul R. Ehrlich†⇊ and Anne H. Ehrlich

We have the smarts, we have the knowledge, we have the desire; let us take back the power that belongs to *us the people* and that -till now- we have very irresponsibly let the establishment use to run and exploit us in the most uncivilized way.

Don't be a stranger..."

What chance was there of you and me meeting
On the same planet, the same century,
With the bad prospect of global warming,
This period of toys and of great hurry.

Against clock and time we run foolishly,
We run against time towards our death,
Like if we, somehow, were in a hurry
To meet Him...or Her, after our last breath!

Don't be a stranger when you meet me, please!
Like you, I've been taught to fear the unknown,
Men and animals, and pain and disease,
Original thoughts, new paths of our own...

Life is a challenge we don't understand,
Rushed by the strong wants we take for reel needs.
The wants torture us and from where I stand,
The real needs are few, please listen and heed.

The fuel for our soul: everywhere we look,
Like the air we breathe and the food we eat,
Been on every lips, said in every book,
And the more we give, the more we shall reap.

That fuel, so precious, and so important,
We can't do without, if we want to live
If we want to grow through every instant,
To remain alert and remain alive,

That fuel we all have is the gift of love
Everybody has to share with others.
Without love from life or from the above,
Nothing makes sense; take my word, brothers...

Roméo Gauvreau, decasyllabic, July 10th, 2013

Conclusion

"Like through a long pregnancy, I have been carrying this book in my heart and soul since 1968-69."

In the introduction, I was using that metaphor to explain the weight of carrying an ideal, a cause, something close to our heart like a mother does a baby... I have finally given birth to that book, after 45 years of that literary pregnancy.

Is it full term, is it normal, all its toes, all its fingers? You are the midwife who has helped me deliver, who has examined the product of my delivery. I hope you consider it an ok baby... In other words, a book that has entertained you for many long hours and, at the same time, has succeeded to provoke in you a reflection on our society and on our school system, in particular. The subject is vast and not easy to treat thoroughly. A lot more could be said about that extremely important pillar of our society.

After we have implanted a humane school system and only then, there will be hope for a real humanistic evolution of society. And that can only happen by the recognition of the importance of stopping the coerced indoctrination of our kids, at home, at church and at school. When, with the best of intentions, we mold kids so they fit in society we perpetuate the *"status quo"*, and the *"status quo"* is falling short of what we should aim at achieving as a society: self-actualization for our kids and a coercion free culture resulting in a democratic freedom that will accompany them in their adult life.

"It is no measure of health to be well adjusted to a profoundly sick society."

Krishnamurti

Having given birth to this literary baby, my task is not over. I'll continue to help it grow and hopefully see to it that it continues to grow in your minds and consciousness to help bring about a new era in the pursuit of a school system that will continue the parents' mission of helping to actualize a new kind of citizen, a citizen with less *"show-offish"* knowledge, but more knowledge of self and of the other, which is the real and only essential knowledge if we want the humanity to finally do a step in the right direction.

I owe you a heartfelt thank you for having accompanied me to the end. I never wrote a sentence without you in mind and how you would receive me.

Say brothers, say sisters,

I Love you, All of you!

Your brother,

Roméo

(rgovro@shaw.ca)

www.ingramcontent.com/pod-product-compliance
Lightning Source LLC
Chambersburg PA
CBHW020509290526
45786CB00002B/532